R Fremlin

The Potato in Farm and Garden

With Chapters on Disease and Special Cultures

R Fremlin

The Potato in Farm and Garden
With Chapters on Disease and Special Cultures

ISBN/EAN: 9783337091224

Printed in Europe, USA, Canada, Australia, Japan

Cover: Foto ©Lupo / pixelio.de

More available books at **www.hansebooks.com**

THE POTATO

IN

FARM AND GARDEN

WITH CHAPTERS ON

DISEASE AND SPECIAL CULTURES

BY

R. FREMLIN

LONDON
"FARM & HOME" OFFICE
"GARDENING ILLUSTRATED" OFFICE
17 FURNIVAL STREET

CONTENTS.

CHAP.		PAGE
I.	Origin—Kinds—Soils	1
II.	Preparation of the Ground for Planting—Manures and their Application	11
III.	Seed Potatoes	20
IV.	The Planting	33
V.	Spring and Summer Cultivation	42
VI.	Potato Disease	49
VII.	Digging and Marketing	75
VIII.	Clamping and Storing	81
IX.	Raising Seedling Potatoes	90
X.	Potato Selection	102
XI.	Forcing Potatoes	105
XII.	Experiments with Potatoes	112
XIII.	Special Cultures :—	
	1. London Market Garden Culture	127
	2. Early Potatoes in Scotland	131
	3. The Main or Late Crop of Potatoes in Scotland	137
	4. How Early Potatoes are Grown in Lancashire	149
	5. Potato Growing in Jersey	153
XIV.	Growing Potatoes for Exhibition	162

THE POTATO.

CHAPTER I.

Origin, Kinds, Soils.—It is not satisfactorily settled who is entitled to the credit of the introduction of the potato. Sir Walter Raleigh, Sir Francis Drake, and Hawkins are all mentioned, but the first named has more claims probably to that honour than either. From being at first regarded as a dish for dessert, like fruit or sweetmeats, it gradually became more generally known and its properties better understood, until now we may regard it as an almost indispensable article of diet for every one, and a useful food for most every kind of stock. Until the eighteenth century it was thought but little of by various writers on the subject.

Much success has been achieved, too, in the development of the potato, those we produce now being far superior to those grown formerly, and at this moment we have such an endless variety of sorts, hundreds in fact, both early and late, that from one year's end to another we can obtain good, sound, and handsome potatoes at what may be called fairly reasonable prices. Mr. Lawson, the author of a work on the vegetables of Scotland, divides the different varieties into three classes : 1, the early, whose leaves and stems decay by the time they are ready to dig, the tubers being fit for immediate use; 2, the large field, of which the foliage does not decay until caught by frost, the tubers requiring to be kept some time before being ready for eating; and 3, late large sorts, adapted for cattle feeding. We are told that in its wild state the potato plant yielded so few tubers that twenty people could well-nigh eat the produce of an acre in one day. In its natural state, too, it was rarely more than 1 in. in diameter and of a very insipid and unpalatable flavour. Now, however, with very good cultivation it sometimes yields 160 sacks and upwards to the acre; in fact, 260 sacks are alleged to have been grown, but, of course, the conditions must have been unusual. The case of Mr. Knight surpasses anything of this kind, for in a paper read before the Horticultural Society many years ago he stated that he had grown 324 sacks per acre of the Ashleaf, and believed nearly half as many more might be grown.

Early Sorts.—Amongst the many early potatoes we may enumerate the following as being worthy of notice, presenting as they do features deserving the attention of growers for market or otherwise. Myatt's Prolific is one that in our opinion more nearly approaches perfection than any we know of. Besides being a good cropper, it comes to the table floury when it is first dug, a quality which, unfortunately, but few young potatoes possess, whilst its flavour is all that can be desired. A similar potato to this is the Early Ashleaf, but no degree of success may be expected with either unless the land be good and well prepared. Although neither runs to haulm as do many sorts, yet if the ground is not up to the mark the yield will be disappointing, as the tubers when full grown are not so large as some other varieties. These kidneys must be farmed high enough to prevent the bulk of the yield turning out little larger than good seed. The Royal or Improved Ashleaf Kidney is early and a good cooker when lifted; it is a strain of the old Ashleaf, but the tubers are generally somewhat smaller. The Hammersmith Kidney crops heavily and has large tubers, and the Early Rose, a pinkish variety, which by some people is much appreciated, on some soils grows really good. Alpha, an American variety, is alleged to be the earliest, as its name implies, but may not be said to have met with universal commendation. Triumph, Extra Early Vermont, Pride of America, and Mona's Pride are all good sorts. The Early Shaw is a potato well known to market gardeners, as also is the Lapstone Kidney, a second early potato, of medium-sized tubers, and a great cropper, also the Ashleaf varieties. The Early Oxford is a potato recommended for its forwardness, whilst the Snowflake, a white, handsome kidney, resembling the Magnum Bonum in appearance, although of a less luxuriant habit of growth, may also almost be classified with our early varieties; it is a heavy cropper.

Second Earlies and Late Sorts.—The International Kidney, and Climax which is a round variety, are both white and of medium growth, as also is the Woodstock Kidney, a good, handsome, cropping potato, suitable for both culinary and exhibition purposes. They all may be reckoned second earlies, and when we have mentioned such sorts as Dalmahoy, Victoria, Champion, Flourball, Surprise. Beauty of Hebron, Trophy, Schoolmaster, white and red Regent, Hero, and the Magnum Bonum above alluded to, we have given a list of both second earlies and late varieties that offers a good choice for any intending planter.

The Dalmahoy is like a Regent in growth, but ripens earlier, with tubers above the medium size; it is a good, useful, and cropping potato. Patterson's Victoria is a strong growing species with medium-sized tubers, rather sunken eyes, and white, firm flesh; a late and heavily cropping variety. The Champion is perhaps at the height of its popularity, and believed by some to be nothing else than the well-known Rock under a new name. Messrs. Carter received an order for 1,000 tons of this potato from the Lord Mayor of London for distribution in Ireland in 1880, value 10,000 guineas. The Flourball is sufficiently well known not to require any special mention. Beauty of Hebron is a comparatively new potato, a rapid grower, of good quality, and handsome; it is a light red-skinned kidney variety. Schoolmaster is a rough, white, round, hardy potato; tubers handsome, haulm short, and a heavy cropper, whilst the Regents are well known for their good cooking qualities and fine flavour. They crop well on good ground, but in Scotland, where they are largely grown, the two or three bad seasons that have occurred the last ten years have greatly checked their cultivation in favour of Champions and Victorias. Magnum Bonum, which has been before the public for some six or seven years, is of exceedingly luxuriant habit, requiring plenty of room between the rows to prevent the haulm all being in a wood, as it were. It is very late, but crops well under good cultivation, some of the tubers being exceedingly handsome. Although it is a good cooker, it is perhaps not so delicately flavoured as some sorts that might be named.

As we do not wish to restrict the choice entirely to the sorts we have named, we give the list of twenty-four varieties which were shown by Mr. Porter four or five years ago at the Paris Exhibition, and for which he obtained the gold medal. The letters and figures opposite to each indicate the sort, stage of earliness, size, and the degree of manuring best adapted for each. Thus, R for round, K for kidney, C for coloured, W for white; 1, 2, and 3, denote first, second, and third earlies, none of them, however, being really late sorts; M, L, and S, signify medium, large, and small respectively whilst x, xx, xxx indicate a rather sparing application, a medium quantity, and a liberal allowance of manure, as the case may be. For example: C. R. (1. M. xxx) means a coloured round potato, first early, of medium size, requiring a heavy supply of manure to produce it properly.

List of twenty-four varieties of potatoes:—

Early Emperor	C. R. (1. M. xxx)
Porter's Excelsior	W. R. (1. M. xxx)
Grampion	C. R. (2. L. xx)
Rector of Woodstock	W. R. (2. M. xxx)
Lye's Favourites	C. R. (2. M. xxx)
Climax	W. R. (2. M. xx)
Radstock Beauty	C. R. (2. M. xxx)
Lady Webster	C. R. (1. S. xxx)
Bresee's Peerless	W. R. (2. M. x)
Alpha	W. R. (1. S. xx)
Schoolmaster	W. R. (3. M. x)
Blanchard	C. R. (2. M. xxx)
Bresee's Prolifie	W. K. (2. M. xx)
Improved Ashtop Fluke	W. K. (1. M. xxx)
International	W. K. (2. M. xx)
Early King	W. K. (2. L. xx)
Model	W. K. (3. L. xx)
Bountiful	C. K. (2. M. xxx)
Keystone	C. K. (3. M. xx)
Snowflake	W. K. (1. S. xxx)
Garibaldi	C. K. (3. M. xxx)
Albion Ashleaf	W. K. (1. S. xxx)
Napoleon	C. K. (3. M. xxx)
Crimson Walnut-leaf	C. K. (3. M. xxx)

Soils for Potatoes.—In the case of such a crop as the potato, which is so affected by local and other considerations, the choice of sorts must be left in a great measure to the gardener or farmer, inasmuch as some that do very well in certain districts upon certain soils would not give satisfactory results everywhere. It would not be easy to find a soil where the potato would not grow, but, like every other vegetable, it has its favourite, and a person would not be prudent to embark in its culture too largely unless that were present. A rich, sandy loam is perhaps as good or a better soil than any; a chalky soil is also fairly good, tubers growing upon either, forming a capital change of seed from one to the other respectively. If some old hedgerow be grubbed up and planted, a heavy yield of potatoes may be looked for where that stood. They are grown also upon peaty or boggy land, where scarcely anything can be made remunerative, also upon a clay soil, but in old turf they seem to revel in a marked degree, enormous tubers being grown therein.

In planting, however, upon this, of course steps must be taken to prevent injury from wireworm, which may be looked for in turf in pretty good force. Although it may be tedious, whenever one shows itself in the process of moving the ground, whether it be in digging, trenching, or ploughing, it should be killed. In any field where they are expected to be met with in any quantity, there should be some-one following the plough to look for them, and some provision made to make off with as many as possible where a man may be trenching or digging by the piece. We have picked up many of these potato marauders and smashed them between our fingers;

but some such plan as giving the ground a good dressing of 4 cwt. to 5 cwt. per acre of salt, or a good sprinkling of lime and soot, must also be adopted, and will produce good results.

It is a highly important matter that the ground be as well drained as possible, because the tubers cannot be expected to have that condition or flavour about them if during their growth they are subjected to the presence of continual dampness, arising from stagnant water. It is alleged by Shirley Hibberd, that a dry, fertile, and mellow soil, free from large stones and exposed to both light and air, is necessary to a potato's perfect development. Any one who has had experience in potato growing must have observed the ill-shaped tubers that come out of a piece of wet, clayey, heavy land, owing, of course, to its being of so close a texture that they could not possibly assume their proper and desired shape.

Writing upon potatoes nearly eighty years ago, a clergyman says: "They should be planted in fresh ground every year. If either fresh or the same seed be planted upon the same soil for two or three years successively, the crops will generally fail, the haulm come up curled and blighted, and the roots will be worm-eaten and cankered. The cause of this may perhaps be assigned. Every species of plant is provided by Nature with pores of such construction and magnitude as are capable of receiving those particles of nourishment only whose dimensions are correspondent to the said pores. Hence every species must receive or imbibe the abovesaid particles only, and reject all others; and, consequently, if the same species be planted or sown upon the same soil for two or three years in succession, the greater part of such particles will be exhausted, and the plants cannot flourish for want of proper nourishment."

Mr. Hibberd above alluded to says further: "The beautiful samples that are seen in winning collections at exhibitions are the produce, generally speaking, of soils that are of a clean, pulverized character, and which while they afford abundant nutriment to the plant, permit the tubers to expand equally in all directions, so that they attain their full size and natural shape quickly, and without encountering obstructions that would mar their beauty. In a lumpy or strong soil the tubers are necessarily misshapen through the impediments to uniform expansion. In a pasty loam or stiff clay the resistance to expansion is equalized, and the uniform compression co-operating with excess of moisture in such soils produces tubers that have the consistence of putty, and to the educated palate are simply uneatable. Hence the selfsame sort, however good initially, may be handsome and eatable when grown on a light, friable, warm, dry soil, but when taken from a stiff clay or badly worked loam will be more or less deformed, and such as to be unfit for any respectable table so far as regards high quality.

"The potato, though peculiar and capricious in constitution, is nevertheless a very accommodating plant. Hence it may be grown with some degree of success, depending, of course, on the nature of the season, on any kind of soil that will produce a mere blade of grass. I have many times lifted crops of 15 tons to 20 tons per acre from low-lying undrained clay land, where in such seasons as 1860 or 1879 the sets would rot in the soil without starting, or at the very best would produce a crop that would not pay for lifting. I have seen excellent crops of smallish potatoes grown on dry mining 'tips' in South Wales, where the rubbish appeared too poor to produce the meanest weed. I have in the disastrous season of 1870 during the months of July and August, eaten the moist delicious Ashleaf kidney potatoes grown in districts of Lancashire, Westmoreland, and Cumberland, where the rainfall averages from 60 in. to 100 in., but where there is no bodyment of water in the soil, and no extremes of heat and cold occur to affect the health of this esculent and sensitive plant. Perfect drainage seems to be the first requisite to success. From the moment the plant becomes waterlogged it has received its deathblow; but, given sufficient depth of soil, and full exposure to the daylight, with free escape of every drop of moisture the plant does not require, and a fair crop commensurate with the conditions may be looked for in a season fairly favourable to vegetation. There is probably no plant in cultivation that can equal the potato in scraping money out of sheer sand, or shale, or starving chalk and limestone."

This last fact may be readily discerned by any one who will take notice of them on the Lancashire coast by the St. George's Channel, where the soil is very sandy, and good crops of potatoes are grown. In a word, no other vegetable probably has such a world-wide cultivation. Every county in England, Wales, and Scotland contributes some, from Rutlandshire and Selkirk with their 385 acres and 224 acres to Lancashire and Yorkshire with their 42,809 acres and 42,164 acres respectively. The returns for 1882, however, show a falling off of some 38,000 acres as compared with 1881, or a decrease of 6·6 per cent. devoted to this crop; but our yield of potatoes may be called equal to some £16,000,000 sterling annually, whilst in 1880 we imported them to the value of nearly £3,000,000 sterling.

CHAPTER II.

Preparation of the Ground for Planting.—It is a very bad plan to attempt growing potatoes on improperly worked land, as is too often the case. Times without number, not only crops of potatoes, but many others, fall far short of expectation, and give little or no satisfaction, for the simple reason that the necessary conditions have not been complied with. This might have been otherwise had the person responsible for the various operations connected with their culture been properly versed in the matter. In some seasons we are precluded from doing very much to our land that we know ought to be, and which we should like to see, done, and, if truth must be spoken, farmers ofttimes have not the wherewithal to expend in the preliminary operations requisite for growing a creditable crop.

The presence of a good lot of manure for the production of a heavy yield of potatoes is a condition that may not seldom be regarded as almost indispensable, although others must be so far observed as to obtain the benefit the manure is designed to give, a proper and a thorough tillage being necessary in conjunction with it in order to secure the heaviest possible returns. Where turf has been trenched or ploughed in there is a coat of manure of itself when the sods have become decomposed, but upon arable land that has been long devoted to potato or other culture, heavy yields can only be looked for where corresponding dressings of manure supplement the most thorough cultivation that can be adopted. We believe some land is as potato sick as other is clover sick, and when digging up time comes the yield is nothing like so heavy as it might be under altered conditions. These remarks apply particularly to the small allotment grounds and Kennedy gardens farmed by our labouring classes, and to small out-of-the-way pieces of land. On the other hand, there can be no question about our being able to crop and recrop the same ground with potatoes to greater advantage than we do were we sufficiently careful to supply the proper manures.

There is no doubt that most all grounds intended for potatoes or other root crops which are put in in the spring of the year, should, wherever practicable, be subjected to the influence of the winter's frosts, which every farmer knows has such a pulverizing effect upon land baulked up deeply and roughly to secure its passing through it and under it. This can be worked down in the spring as the time for planting draws near, and on light soils especially, a little cultivation (if the weather be dry) will bring the land into a suitable state for drawing out the drills. Fields with great hard clods of earth are not those that will give a satisfactory yield of good-shaped tubers, so that it is essential such preliminary steps be adopted as shall get the land as fine as is necessary, but, of course, we need not strive to obtain a season such as swedes or turnips require. An extra ploughing, harrowing, and rolling would often be labour and money well expended in some of our varied preparatory operations, not only for this, but also for other crops.

One special merit belonging to a potato crop, and which ought not to be overlooked, is its great value as a cleaning agency. During the late spring and summer, even till the crop is raised, peculiar opportunities are offered for ridding the land of many noxious weeds, which of necessity stand and seed among many other things through inability to get at and destroy them without injury to such crops. A century ago potatoes were claimed as being useful in meliorating the ground, and were recommended to be introduced regularly in the rotation of crops on good light soils.

Modes of Growing.—So many varying conditions are met with in potato cultivation that one or other of the many systems of planting is adopted as each particular case arises. There are the lazy-oed system, digging the ground and putting in with the spade, digging the ground and then dibbling the potatoes in, ploughing them in, which is an operation that is well known, and last of all, and unquestionably best of all, there is the common practice of drawing out drills either by the hand or, when there is a good acreage to be got in, by employing horse-power. The first system is best adapted to some of the boggy and peaty undrained soils, and is practised more especially in Ireland and in Cheshire. The plan is to level the ground by digging a shallow trench around and through the plot, so as to mark out a series of quadrangular beds. Upon these the sets are planted and covered up with soil from the trenches, which are thus deepened and make a more or less complete system of drainage. Digging the ground with the spade or the spud, or fork (which latter implement is better if the ground is not too pulverized), and planting the sets as the digging proceeds, is more of a gardener's plan, and has the advantage of leaving the ground planted without being trodden upon after being dug. The dibbling system may also be employed in gardens as it is sometimes in the field; but we are not in favour with it, since the time spent in making the holes with the dibber might, in our opinion, be better employed in simply placing the sets in properly drawn drills, which we shall say more about farther on. To grow potatoes successfully after being dibbled, it is absolutely necessary that the ground be thoroughly friable and well worked, so that the dibble leaves nothing at all like a walled cell behind it, which will naturally offer some obstruction to the set when sprouting. Added to this it may, in very wet weather, induce the water to lie round the sets, which is about as undesirable a state of affairs as can be well conceived.

The plan of ploughing the sets in has the merit, with plenty of strength at hand, of getting over the ground, and of insuring fairly straight rows of potatoes by-and-by; but there is nothing that equals the practice of drawing good wide drills with the bouting plough, and with the same implement splitting these bouts, thus throwing back a good quantity of crumby soil into the drills over the sets. The field can afterwards be harrowed down across the drills with a light horse; in fact, where practicable, light, small-footed horses are best for *healing* in also, so that the sets may not be injured through being trodden upon. It should, moreover, not be forgotten that the more space they have and the less obstruction potatoes meet with during their growth, so much the better for the crop; therefore great clods, and large stones near them is just what should be avoided if possible. Provided, however, the ground all about the sets be fairly fine, it is not so material that the surface be in that state.

Manures and their Application.—The crop of

potatoes is greatly determined by the quantity and quality of the manure allowed. Some of the kidney varieties, although not luxuriant in their habit like the Magnum Bonum, are, nevertheless, gross feeders, that is, they require very liberal treatment to produce a crop, and it would be safe to say that in nine cases out of ten unfavourable results with these arise through a too scanty allowance of manure. Some other sorts, however, will give a good yield with more moderate supplies. Old pastures broken up and planted with potatoes furnish something that just suits them, but unfortunately there seems to be a kind of superstitious reverence surrounding them (we do not know why), hedged about as they are with most stringent conditions, so that the occupier of such worn-out pasture land is debarred the benefit he would obtain from breaking them up and taking a crop of potatoes and afterwards corn, and duly laying them down again, whilst the owner on his part loses the increase in the value of his land that such treatment would most certainly confer upon it.

Better than any artificial manure that we know of for producing crops of potatoes is farmyard dung, which, generally speaking, should be used pretty liberally, especially on poor land, because due regard should be had for the succeeding crop. Where early varieties have been grown, a green crop may be raised at once, and ploughed in at Michaelmas or a little later on for wheat, which probably is as good as anything to follow potatoes, and if justice has been done to the ground during the spring and summer and at digging-up time, there should be a good clean seed bed for the wheat sowing.

There is no doubt much to be said for an autumn manuring of land intended for spring planting of potatoes, inasmuch as the dung during that period becomes more incorporated with the soil, and, after the necessary tillage immediately previous to planting, is presented to the seed in a condition more easily appropriated than that put in the ground at planting time. On heavy soils, too, the ploughing in of a coat of rough dung is of use in keeping the ground somewhat hover, thus assisting the drainage and the action of the frosts. Still, we must not overlook the fact of the loss which it sustains in the ground during the winter, particularly if a wet one, a consideration that induces us to prefer spring manuring. The manure itself should be adapted to the ground. For instance, on a dry, hot, sandy soil it may be in a much more advanced stage of decomposition than where heavy and somewhat tenacious land is to be dealt with; in both instances a maximum of benefit will thus be obtained. Even where no intermediate crop is to be taken, ploughing in manure all over the ground should not be dispensed with; whilst in the case of market gardening, the ground *must* be mended all over, in addition to that put in the drills with the sets, in which case also the land should determine the quality of the manure, as mentioned above.

It seems to be an open question, whether the sets or the manure should be first put into the drills, but we incline strongly to and adopt the plan of putting the dung on the top of the potatoes. Several ends are attained by this system; the dung prevents the earth pressing on them too tightly, thus assisting the development of the tubers, and providing sustenance for them as they grow. If the manure is put at the bottom of the drill and the sets upon it, the rain carries the virtue of the manure away from the tubers; whereas, by placing the manure last, as the haulm grows through it, the young potatoes keep forming therein. A third recommendation is the protection a good coat of manure offers to the sets as the horse walks down the ridges when healing them in; and lastly, in the case of severe frosts, which sometimes occur in March, after perhaps very early plantings have been made, the dung on the top secures them from danger better than does the soil by itself. We do not advise the use of thoroughly rotted, heavy dung in the rows, but that in a medium state that has been simply thrown once into a mixen. It is not a bad plan to sprinkle a little soot in the bottom and on the sides of the drills; some use guano with the dung; rape-dust, again, is a useful artificial, alone, at the rate of 10 cwt. to 12 cwt. per acre, besides which kainit, dissolved bones, and several other manures may be used with varying degrees of success. Two years ago we saw tried, side by side with dung, an artificial recommended and sold by a London merchant, but the results were not so satisfactory as were expected, and would not induce us to depend too much upon them alone. On sandy soils or in very dry seasons superphosphate and potash salts would no doubt give much better results than many other artificials. Ordinary wood ashes from bakers' ovens are very good for potatoes, whilst lime and salt are also spoken of as a manure, but we have had no experience with the latter for this crop.

The influence exercised upon potatoes by merely planting them on a totally different soil is considered so beneficial, that any grower would always do well to procure his seed grown in as diverse a one as possible to that he intends planting. One by no means small grower, who has had eighteen years' experience of them in the Midland Counties, says he has proved a good change of seed to be worth a ton of potatoes per acre. We attach importance to this changing from one soil to another for the sake of the potato itself, as it no doubt tends to its invigoration, or at any rate to the retarding of its degeneration. Where, from any circumstance, a field is frequently planted with them it will be well sometimes to change even the variety itself. Beyond this the less often a piece of ground is cropped with them the better it is, although we believe this matter is paid too little attention to.

CHAPTER III.

Seed Potatoes.—Although we have been engaged growing this vegetable for the last three hundred years, there is still a diversity of opinion upon many of the cardinal points of its cultivation. Whether the seed should be whole or cut, how many eyes should be left on a set, how large the seed ought to be, and when it is best to plant, are all undecided points, or if any or all these details are determined to the satisfaction of potato growers generally, yet is their practical application so varied, that no work upon potatoes would be complete without their being properly discussed.

Having decided in the fall of the year upon the ground for our spring planting, proper steps should be taken for bringing it into the best state possible when the time comes for putting the potatoes in. It should, therefore, be balked up deeply, so as to expose as large a surface as well can be to the agency of the frosts. This is not so important upon very light soils, as one or two ploughings in the spring and the usual harrowings will give as fine a tilth as is necessary. Many large growers very possibly make a practice of reserving their own seed where the conditions are favourable for doing so, and on farms of very diverse soils this is better than having to purchase just when wanted, sometimes at very high prices. If, moreover, care has been taken with the crop when growing, and at digging-up time, the seed ought to be pretty true, a point we do not think receives the attention it deserves. Any one, however, who is not provided with seed of his own growing must, as soon as the winter is fairly over, give due attention to the matter. Possibly some well-known farmer at a distance, or, better still, near home, has some reliable seed to dispose of, grown perhaps upon as different a soil as would be found a couple of hundred miles away. It will be better to obtain this than sending to a regular potato dealer a long way off, all other things being equal, as in the transit of such bulky and heavy ware as potatoes the carriage must never be lost sight of. For example, the ground to be planted is perhaps of a light, sandy nature, and two miles off it is as chalky as possible; or it may happen that a neighbour has grown a crop of healthy potatoes upon a gravelly soil, and the field to be planted is of a clayey character. In cases of this kind better conditions for a good crop are offered to a grower than if he had seed from the other end of the country, if it had been raised on similar land to his own.

In potato, as in other cultivation, it must ever be borne in mind, that particular varieties of fruit, hops, or what not have their favourite localities and soils, and what perhaps succeeds well here may not unlikely a few miles distant more nearly approach failure. Local observation must be a powerful factor in deciding upon the sort most likely to turn out well. A case in point is presented by the Early Rose, which is said to grow upon the light land round

Albury, in Surrey, better than anywhere in the county, cooking floury from the first until potatoes come again. On the sand, however, at Woking, a few miles distant, they are apt when boiled to come to the table waxy.

The Sets.—We like healthy, medium-sized sets for planting, say as large as a hen's egg, although we have seen a good yield of potatoes from seed no bigger than walnuts. In general, however, we advise no one to set his ground with the smallest potatoes unless there is no option, or he has some new and valuable variety which he is desirous of increasing as largely and speedily as possible, and therefore plants anything and everything for a year or two till he has attained his object. We hope we are all so far advanced in our knowledge of potato growing in these days to feel that the following remarks, which were written many years ago, are not very applicable to ourselves; still, there is a hint or two therein of sufficient value to justify their reproduction here:—

"Intelligent farmers are particular, and even curious, in the choice of their seed grain. But in respect to potatoes chosen for planting, they are mostly the rubbish of the crop. Upon what principle this method is adopted it is hard to imagine, unless it be to save the inconsiderable trouble of cutting the sets. The seed potatoes saved in like manner from the crop of this rubbish, it appears obvious, must be continually degenerating, till at length they will no more answer the trouble and expense of cultivation. Hence farmers are driven to the necessity of purchasing their seed potatoes at an expensive rate from distant parts of the kingdom; the supply also is precarious, and good seasons for planting are frequently lost."

It seems in the selection of our seed we are too apt to place size before shape, and so long as a potato appears large enough for planting it is thrown into the seed lump. For instance, if we take a Magnum Bonum, which just now stands in the front rank as being a prolific cropper; in overhauling a clamp of this sort we shall find very varied shaped potatoes therein, some being of a rounded character, and others kidney-shaped, as they should be. If they are all passed on for planting, the natural tendency must be to perpetuate these distinctive features, so that by-and-by a clamp of potatoes comes to present an irregular and unhandsome appearance. This, too, may become more marked by setting ugly, ill-shaped seed, that favours neither the round nor the kidney varieties; such specimens will turn up sometimes, but should be taken into the kitchen, or otherwise made off with, but never planted. We do not wish to convey the impression that like will readily produce like in this case—*e.g.*, that kidney-shaped seed will yield an entire crop of similarly formed potatoes; but a little persistence in the selection of seed, with the same special characteristics for a few years, will doubtless tend to the propagation of those possessing such features; and we believe by a careful elimination of any that do not come up to the required standard we might in time establish more regularly-formed and handsome varieties. The result, however, will always in a great measure depend upon the well or badly cultivated state of the ground, as alluded to in the last chapter. Want of time is no doubt a great cause of seed being used that should be otherwise disposed of, for in the hurry of picking over the clamps the grower is more anxious to see the work progressing than he is about the exact character of his seed. Another reason, probably quite as valid, if not more so, is that of oversight, he never having given that thought and attention to the subject that is exercised in respect to other branches of cultivation upon the farm.

In order to maintain anything like a standard of perfection in any one thing, there is doubtless a need for constant vigilance, and if the bad types are not kept under, we come in due course to find our crop has deteriorated either in quantity or quality, perhaps in both. A writer alluding to a new variety of potato speaks of its treatment thus: "For the first year or two special care is devoted to its culture, and to the tubers after they are lifted. We speak in glowing terms of this new variety; we admire the beauty of its foliage, the symmetrical form and fine texture and flavour of its tubers, and, above all, its extra cropping qualities. But in a few years, in all probability, it has fallen to the level of an average variety, and we say the potato has degenerated. That it does degenerate there is no doubt, but is there any one subject either in the animal or vegetable kingdom but would have degenerated or, more probably, ceased to exist under such treatment as the potato has received at our hands? It has been the practice to select for propagation the refuse of the potato heap; small, ugly, immature, ill-shaped tubers have been considered good enough for seed; and when the result has not met our expectation, we have raised the cry that the potato is degenerating. In carrying out this practice for years was it possible to arrive at any other result?" Nothing is gained by planting the largest potatoes one can procure, as this is only so much waste. It would be quite possible to use up a ton and more of seed in planting an acre, although the proper disposition of half that quantity would result in quite as heavy a yield; therefore, on the score of economy, no more should be planted than is necessary to produce a maximum weight.

Cutting Sets.—If time were but of little moment, such as may be the case in gentlemen's gardens, a few potatoes may be made to go a very long way. There is no necessity whatever for half or even a quarter of the eyes being left upon the sets. This is an established fact, the knowledge of which enables successful experiments to be made with them, and where great care is used in cutting a potato, leaving a fair portion of it with the eye, a dozen or two of any very special sort may be made to produce almost a fabulous yield. In the case of the medium-sized seed, such as before described, perhaps we cannot much improve upon the old-fashioned and tried plan of putting in the sets whole, but where the seed runs larger than a duck's egg the knife should be passed through it once from the bunch of eyes downwards. Where they are very large, each half may then be similarly divided. It is not a bad plan where they have not been cut to take off a horizontal slice with the knife, just to remove the bunch of eyes, as plenty will then be left on other parts of the set which will receive all the support of the potato.

It is not everyone who is much in favour with cutting sets of kidney potatoes, but we see no reason why a kidney should not be divided the same as another variety, provided it be large enough. Whenever cut sets are used they should not be planted for a day or two after being prepared, in which case they will not go into the ground with the juice exuding from their newly cut sides. Hot lime, however, sprinkled over them to absorb this moisture, prevent decay, and attacks of insects, is recommended, and plant at once, but we have had no experience with it, and should hesitate somewhat before adopting the practice. Mr. Crews, in his work upon potatoes, says kidneys never should be cut, and assigns the following reasons : " By cutting the sets are so weakened that many perish through exhaustion or dry rot, and those that grow are generally weak, and not nearly so productive as those tubers that are planted whole; again, potatoes set in their entirety stand wet or cold, heat and drought, much better than those subjected to cutting.

They are also not so susceptible to the ravages of the botrytis, besides enabling the plants to grow more equally or evenly." Another writer upon the potato remarks that he is led from experience to conclude that whole sets produce a greater bulk of potatoes, and are more able to contend against disease than those raised from cut sets. On the other hand, it is certain that if a large potato be cut into sets, the yield therefrom will be much greater than if it were planted whole; and if we were going to raise as many as possible from say a kidney weighing 6 oz., we should have no hesitation in dividing it into two sets at least.

As a proof of the value of this contention we ourselves grew 35 gallons of Magnum Bonum a few years ago from 1 gallon of seed, but we used cut sets in order to do so, and gave them plenty of room. Whilst writing this we have before us the statement of one who has this very season had good proof of the value of cutting, and we give it here: "From some very large specimens of Magnum Bonum I, last spring, selected the handsomest tuber, cut it into sets, and planted it with the following results: The crop from this one potato just raised weighs 95 lb., and consists of 190 tubers; 84 weigh over $\frac{1}{2}$ lb. each. Of these 74 are over $\frac{3}{4}$ lb., 28 over 1 lb., 8 over $1\frac{1}{4}$ lb., 2 weigh 1 lb. 6 oz., 2, 1 lb. 7 oz., and the largest turns the scale at 1 lb. 10 oz. There were no signs of disease, and all the tubers but three were of good shape." It would be interesting to know just how many this tuber would have grown

if planted whole. A person at Henham, a few years
ago, hearing various opinions respecting the supposed
advantage of planting large sets of potatoes, resolved
to settle it to his own satisfaction by giving both
large and small sets a fair trial, placing them side by
side. He chose a peck of the largest American Rose
variety, the measure holding twenty potatoes, and
on March 11 planted them 1 yard apart each way
across a vegetable quarter. He also planted six
rows of the same variety about the size of a hen's
egg, and found that, although the large sets had the
advantage of being in the outside row, their produce
was the lightest of all. The proportion of small
potatoes from the large sets was also much greater
than from the small, as they sent up a greater
quantity of haulm; on the other hand, the potatoes
from the small sets were nearly all over the average
size.

Mr. R. Beale, writing in the *Live Stock Journal*
upon this subject, says: "It is supposed that there
is in the potato a separate set of fine tissues or vein-
like threads for each eye. Admitting this fact, the
next question is, 'Where are they situated?' In
order to arrive at something like a conclusion on
this point I tried an experiment with convincing
results. It was carried out in the following manner
in the summer of 1879. First, it should be stated
that the variety of potato called the American Early
Rose cannot be put to a better use perhaps than to
work out experiments. It is well suited for that
purpose. Early Rose was the subject of the present

test. Selecting a dozen average sized tubers, they were formed into groups of three each, first being reduced to but one eye. Those of Group No. 1 were planted whole in some well-prepared ground. Group No. 2 were cut in half across the middle, and the halves that contained the eyes were planted next. Group No. 3 had two-thirds of the tuber cut off, drawing the knife again at right angles with the length of the tubers, and planting the lesser portions containing the eye. Group No. 4 were cut in the same way as the third group, and were again reduced by having a circular piece taken off from the outer edge, reducing it to half the size of No. 3. Not much difference could be observed in the first, second, and third groups during the growth of the foliage, but the fourth showed a marked difference from the first, being always of a more delicate and weakly appearance. By the time that the first three groups had formed their full-grown foliage the fourth had ceased to grow, and had begun to die off, two of them, in fact, shrinking quite away. When the produce was lifted all yielded tubers, but those from the fourth group were decidedly smaller, but weight was considered the fairest test, and accordingly out came the scales. No. 1 weighed 9 lb. 10 oz.; No. 2, 9 lb. $10\frac{1}{2}$ oz.; No. 3, 8 lb. 2 oz.; and No. 4 weighed 4 lb. 11 oz.

"Not being satisfied with the results of this trial, a different system was followed in 1880, which was as follows: For the sake of comparing the weights the same numbers were taken and classed again in four groups, the cutting now being in a longitudinal direction. An eye near the point of the tuber was again reserved in each instance, and the cuts approaching this eye at certain distances. The three tubers of the first group were planted whole. The second group had a section of about one-third taken off with a knife in a slanting direction, cutting from about 1 in. from the eye, and finishing the cut at the centre of the stem end of the tuber. The third group were cut in exactly the same direction, and the knife was then reversed, and another third of the tuber was taken off, leaving the eye in the centre of the broad end of a wedge-shaped piece of potato. The fourth division were cut in the same manner as the last, with the difference that on each occasion the knife was inserted at a distance of only $\frac{1}{2}$ in. from the eye on each side. After this a third cut was made across the length of the wedge at a distance of one-third of its length from the broad end. The cut sets were dusted over with very fine sifted dust from dry soil, containing a small quantity of sulphur, and then dried. Sulphur was used to counteract the mildew that must have set in in the first experiment, and that showed itself in the smallest cuttings.

"When ready the prepared sets were planted, and closely observed. The fourth group again soon began to show signs of weakness, though not to the extent that appeared in the first instance. The leaves were small and the stems very short and thin, but they kept colour till the growth was nearly completed, and then seemed rapidly to ripen. In August, when the potatoes were all dug up, it was found that the first and second groups were again about equal; the third lot were also nearly approaching, being only 13 oz. short, whilst the fourth group weighed less than half the weight of the first.

"These two trials convincingly proved that in cutting potatoes for sets, enough width and depth of flesh must be left around the eye that is intended to produce a crop. It also proved that when the cuts are made too near to the eye, or when the portion left is very thin, the eye is weakened in some way or other. We may, therefore, feel satisfied that the tissues or fibres of the tuber are distinct for each eye, and that they extend to at least an inch from the base of the eye into the tuber.

"This important matter, size of sets, will have received some light from the foregoing account of experiments of cutting. It is, however, necessary to advise that in all instances where land is heavy and wet it is better to use tubers cut in half, for the simple reason that, as the old sets are all sure to decay in such soil, the sooner they are gone the better it will be for what is left. The largest and, perhaps, the best potato grower of the present day (Mr. William Kerr) has a strong partiality for small potatoes for sets; and he also puts them through a systematic course of preparation from the time that they are first dug out of the ground. Any ordinary potato grower, walking across Mr. Kerr's potato fields in August, would hold up his hands at what appears to be gross wastefulness and extravagance, but which is in reality systematic economy. The smallest tubers are made use of, and all are thoroughly greened before leaving the ground.

"But it may be laid down as a rule that any tuber that produces an eye or eyes of sufficient stoutness and vigour is as good as can be desired for planting, no matter whether it be of large, medium, or small size. Still, I have always found that average-sized tubers of the round varieties are best when cut, and that the same applies to all the kidney-shaped kinds that have their eyes distributed over the surface. One thing, however, is certain, and that is, that the further the eyes are sprouted—providing they have sufficient stoutness and colour—the less fear is there of doing any harm by cutting the tuber. A good plan, therefore, of multiplying any particular variety is to get all the eyes well pushed that will do so by keeping the tubers in moist heat—say in a box of leaf-mould in a hotbed or pit—before cutting up the tubers.

"Any who wish to satisfy themselves that the quantity is affected by the size of the sets, can easily try the following plan: At planting time divide the sets of any particular kind into four lots, thus: Count off say twenty-one of the largest tubers; cut seven of these in half, and there will be then fourteen sets of each. Next, pick out twenty-one of the smallest tubers, and again cut seven, taking care, of course, to leave eyes on each of the cut parts. Now, weight for weight at planting time, the cut sets will decidedly go farthest, and the grower will also find that, root for root at lifting time, the produce of the cut sets will be the heavier." Any grower who still prefers to plant whole sets can, of course, have his home-grown potatoes sorted so as to avoid any waste, but it happens that in purchasing seed there are found some amongst them that it seems sheer extravagance to set whole. This, at least, is our experience. It may just be remarked in passing that the cutting should be done with a thin-bladed knife, which passes through the potato more easily, and is not so liable to break the set, which during the cutting should be held with the stem down.

CHAPTER IV.

The Planting.—Of course where there is any breadth of ground to be put in, drawing the drills by the hand is quite out of the question, although for garden planting or irregular patches of ground where horse labour cannot well be employed, the old three-pronged hoe is a most serviceable tool, either for drawing out the drills, healing in the potatoes, or earthing them up later on.

We are strongly of opinion that the cultivation of this useful vegetable is not properly understood in so far as the space allowed for each plant is concerned. Before the haulm is full grown until the crop is dug up, one sees the plants in a crowded condition, conducive to the ills they are subject to, and opposed to their due productiveness and proper development. A parallel is found in the overcrowded, ill-ventilated tenements that exist in London and other large towns, prolific sources of all that is bad. Everyone has seen potatoes of robust habit, where the haulm somewhat resembled a green wood, obstructing the free current of air that should pass between the rows. Perhaps there is nothing that more promotes the spread of blight than the inability of the plant to free itself from the dampness which hangs about on the foliage during wet weather. If at planting time this were borne in mind, and an extra 6 in. or 12 in. were allowed between the rows, we should have better crops of potatoes in every way. The horses and the cart wheels could more easily be kept out of the drills while the work was proceeding, as the ridges would not be so sharp. There would be more space to properly work the horse hoe, and more mould could be found for earthing up, rendering it unnecessary to exercise economy in this important operation—fearing that whilst drawing sufficient soil to one row we rob the other, as is now sometimes the case when either row is earthed up as it should be. We are borne out in these observations by practice, for when experimenting with them we have found splendid crops result from giving plenty of room, and any one may test this for himself. Let, for instance, a row be planted somewhere by itself, or where it will have the whole benefit of a yard of unoccupied ground on either side—in other words, where the next row is 6 ft. off—and the great yield by-and-by will show that they are unfairly treated in the ordinary way. We dug up a bountiful crop a few years ago by adopting this plan, and we have even seen 2 bushels of potatoes produced from five medium-sized tubers cut into some half a score of sets, and planted in squares 6 ft. each way, with plenty of good mould.

The sort of potato planted must determine the distance between the rows; a Magnum Bonum, for example, requires nearly double the space of an early variety that runs to but little top. Scarcely any sort should be planted less than $2\frac{1}{2}$ ft. between the rows and 1 ft. between the sets; better to increase these distances to 3 ft. and 15 in. respectively than the reverse. Those varieties that are disposed to throw a profusion of haulm must be allowed considerably more space, say 1 ft. extra between the rows, and another 3 in. or 4 in. therein; whilst the Magnum Bonum ought to be $4\frac{1}{2}$ ft. to 5 ft. apart, and from 18in. to 20 in. from set to set. Obviously the quantity of seed is affected very materially by considerations of this kind; so also is its expense, and the despatch, moreover, with which an extended acreage may be dug up greatly promoted, although the labour of hoeing and earthing might equal that in the case of rows half that distance apart. All these points, especially in these hard times, are such as a farmer cannot afford to overlook. Whilst we have not seen the plan tried, we believe the results, in a cropping point of view, of placing the sets diagonally in the drills would prove satisfactory, although the planting might take longer. For example, in the case of potatoes of a fairly robust habit of growth, suppose the drills were drawn a yard apart, and in them the sets were laid a yard apart also—the first set in each alternate drill being started at 18 in. from the ends, thus forming a series of triangles over the field—we believe the yield obtained from a plant of this kind would be large; allowing, say 3 lb. to each root, it would give upwards of eighty-six sacks per acre.

In limited spaces on good ground, a writer on potatoes recommends the planting of both early and late varieties in alternate rows $2\frac{1}{2}$ ft. apart, so that the strong and late variety may have all the ground after the early ones are dug; there will thus be abundance of pulverized soil for earthing up if required. In carrying out this it will be necessary to dig the first crop clean, to prevent any mixing of the sorts, which may easily occur, and sometimes entail considerable inconvenience. One other advantage of wide planting which more nearly concerns growers for market is the opportunity it affords for intercropping, inasmuch as many plants have to be got out of the seed-bed into their permanent quarters before the potatoes are off. In digging up the potatoes (we allude now particularly to early varieties) a few weeks later on, such plants as have been got out and are becoming well established are much benefited by the operation, if only the necessary care be exercised so as not to tread upon or otherwise injure them.

The depth at which potatoes are best planted must in a great measure be regulated by the time of year they are put in. Those planted at the end of February, for example, need to be put in deeper than others set two months later on. A covering of earth 2in. or 3in. deep, with March in prospect, would afford but scant protection from the severe frosts we sometimes experience, even in the south of England, in that month. For very late plantings, however, it is not so important to cover them so deeply; but from 2 in. or 3 in. to 5 in. or 6 in. may be taken as the extreme limit either way, always allowing them more depth in light than heavy soils, and reducing the depth slightly as the season advances.

An acquaintance of ours who has had considerable experience in potato growing recommends the earthing up at the time of planting as a saving of expense, and as affording shelter to the spring frosts, his so treated during the past season being scarcely touched, whilst many of his neighbours had the haulm nipped, and we have been told that this practice was general in Canada several years ago. One other consideration, however, that arises from this system is the facility it offers for transplanting any vegetables that may require shifting before potatoes planted in the ordinary way are ready to earth up, an operation that clearly could not be performed after the spaces between the rows are filled. Whilst we adduce this in behalf of this particular feature in potato growing, yet we consider the balance of advantages favours the custom generally in vogue, that of earthing during the summer when the haulm is far enough advanced to require it. The depth at which the sets are buried when earthed up at planting must have a tendency to retard their growth somewhat, and the whole plant is deprived later on of the benefit accruing from the pulverized soil thrown around and against it.

Before discussing the time for planting, we may add that, where ravages are expected from wireworm, it is not a bad plan to put something in the rows to attract them, so that they may be secured and destroyed. Round newly planted hops in some old pasture that has been broken up a piece of potato answers the purpose of a kind of trap, but among potatoes themselves pieces of rape cake are said to be a capital bait for these pests. These can be examined from time to time, and the worms killed, even if the cake itself does not kill them.

Time to Plant.—As a rule we believe potatoes are put in some weeks later than they should be. This practice is attended with more than one evil. The clamps are kept healed up several days longer than is good either for the seed or the ware, and the former particularly gets injured in the handling. When potatoes have been kept in a fair temperature all the winter, and the clamp upon being opened reveals many of them shooting, it is an evidence they should be in the ground. The rubbing off of these shoots, which is almost inevitable in the sorting, carriage to the field, and planting, is so much damage done them, and the crop is affected thereby; although if it were the weakly shoots only that got destroyed during the process, whilst the strong ones were all left intact, the sets would be doubtless rather benefited than otherwise by their removal. In addition to this, a potato that has thrown out considerable shoots while in the clamp has exhausted a part of its energy under unfavourable conditions, and cannot afterwards be regarded as in a thoroughly sound and healthy state. A further consideration which should carry more weight than it apparently does, is the increased liability potatoes have to blight the longer they are out in the fields. Frequently, if the seed were given a better or earlier start in the spring, the tubers would attain to such a degree of maturity that we might oftener do something with them before the blight sets in severely, as it too frequently does.

We do not believe in autumn planting for potatoes, although we admit that by planting thus early they are put into the ground with all the virtue they possess, and, other things being equal, are of much greater value than some planted in the spring, which, having been packed too thickly, and having remained too long in the clamp have sprouted, and been injured as mentioned above. The result is that from sickly and weakened sets the crop is not satisfactory. On the other hand, when planting thus early there remains the risk of using some which may be so slightly attacked with disease as to escape detection, but which would be quickly noticed in the spring. Added to this there must be taken into consideration the loss in value that the manure sustains through remaining in the ground all the winter months; and, lastly, the land loses in a measure the benefits arising from the pulverizing effects of the frost, which benefits, had it been properly prepared for a spring planting, it would have secured to the full. I might also add that the tubers, being so many extra weeks, and even months, have necessarily a severer gauntlet to run through such pests as their great enemy the wireworm, whilst the ground must necessarily get beaten down tightly with the winter rains, a condition adverse to the growth of the tubers. These are the disadvantages surrounding autumn planting. As there can be little doubt that spring-planted potatoes produce a crop fit to dig up about the same time as those planted months previously, the only question is so to preserve the seed during the autumn and winter, that it may be put into the ground at the proper time in spring in a healthy and unimpaired state, and there is no insurmountable difficulty attending this.

It may be interesting here to give the result of the latest experiments of Mr. James Howard, M.P., who, in November 1881, and at the end of March last year planted 28 lb. of the following sorts side by side and the same distance between the rows, 32 in. in the case of strong growing, and 28 in. in those of Ashleaf varieties.

Variety.	Spring planted.	Autumn planted.	Date of lifting.
Improved Ashleaf ....produced	147 lb.	191 lb.	July 21
Woodstock Kidney .... ,,	322 lb.	385 lb.	July 20
Fillbasket .... ,,	432 lb.	330 lb.	July 25
Reading Hero .... ,,	375 lb.	370 lb.	Aug. 16
Reading Abbey .... ,,	492 lb.	370 lb.	Aug. 10
Early Hammersmith (Ashleaf) ,,	458 lb.	483 lb.	July 21
Magnum Bonum .... ,,	504 lb.	509 lb.	Sept. 9
Scotch Champion .... ,,	552 lb.	654 lb.	Sept. 9

It will be seen from the above that while some sorts gave larger yields, the reverse was the case with regard to others; but in every case the drawbacks attending autumn planting must be taken account of. The losses at times connected with November planting have been found disastrous, and it would not do to rely too much upon the experiments extending over such an exceptionally mild winter as that of 1881–2. This particular feature, however, of autumn *versus* spring planting of potatoes will doubtless be satisfactorily decided in a few years' time.

Generally speaking, in the southern counties of England there is no time better than March for potato planting, but in the midland and northern districts it may be deferred a little. As a fact, from the end of February until May, potato planting is going on, but, as we remarked before, very many should be put in some weeks earlier. If the ground can be got into good tilth, early sorts intended for market may be planted at the end of February, but for ordinary purposes the second and third weeks in March are as good a time as any, and we do not like to see the planting protracted all through April, even into May, till about the time that many of the tops of the early planted ones are peeping through the ground. Regarding the quantity of seed per acre, it will be seen that that is determined by its size and the distance which the rows are apart, and likewise by the thickness the sets are placed therein. For instance, a field with drills $2\frac{1}{2}$ ft. from centre to centre and the sets placed at 1 ft. apart, would require exactly double the quantity of seed that another of equal area would take with rows 4 ft. apart and the sets 15 in., if the sets were the same size in both cases. Supposing they averaged eight to the pound, then about $19\frac{1}{2}$ cwt. would be required per acre in the former case, and almost half a ton in the latter.

CHAPTER V.

Spring and Summer Cultivation.—The cultivation of the potato after planting is comparatively easy, the chief point to aim at being the continual and free growth of the plant from the time it shows itself until it ripens and dies away. Between the planting and the appearance of haulm above the ground, a gentle harrowing with a pair of light harrows is very beneficial, as it destroys many seedlings that are certain to precede it; it, moreover, assists the haulm in coming through the ground by breaking the crust which time and the elements have been forming the few weeks previous. Some judgment must plainly be exercised, as a too profuse or deep harrowing when many of the shoots are within half an inch of the surface, will do more harm than good; but a judicious breaking of just the crusty surface a week or two before the haulm shows itself, is safe and prudent. The harrow has been used after the haulm is in sight, but notwithstanding, perhaps, there are in nine out of ten fields many more stems than are required for the production of a crop of potatoes, we deprecate the indiscriminate destruction of however few of them which such a practice would cause.

Spring Frosts.—Where practicable, some attention should be paid to the early growing potatoes—that is, those whose tops make their appearance long before frosts are over. Everyone has seen the haulm of a promising row of early potatoes cut by a frost in May, which naturally receives a check in proportion to the degree of cold. Over an extended acreage, of course, this cannot well be provided against, but, in gardens, a little earth drawn over the precocious stems puts them temporarily out of danger; whilst after the haulm comes up from one end of the row to another, shelter must be afforded in some other way. Some loose, light straw or litter may be spread, or pea boughs laid over carefully, and taken off before the haulm is high enough to get bruised in their removal. The weather during the dangerous month of May must be watched, so that any special precaution that appears necessary can be taken. We have heard of pouring cold water over the haulm in the very early morning to thaw the white frost, so that the ill-effects of the sun may be neutralized—no doubt a very good thing. The adoption of some such expedient as this becomes more urgent where the potatoes are in a valley, or rather where they do not catch the rays of the rising sun. The more imperceptibly the thaw takes place upon any vegetation through the sun's action, the greater will be the immunity from damage; hence the necessity, where possible, of always having an eye to site whenever planting anything of a choice and tender nature, whether it be fruit or vegetables, so that danger from late frosts may be as far as practicable prevented. It may also be remarked here, that independently of the frost, a little soot sprinkled along the rows when the haulm is nicely up is a good thing, or a little nitrate of soda may be sown broadcast.

Horse Hoeing.—As soon as the rows can be distinctly seen, the horse-hoe or brake must be kept frequently at work, which will not only destroy any weeds as fast as they appear, but greatly promote the healthy development of the haulm above and the tubers under the surface. Concurrently with this, the plate hoe must be used to keep the ground clear between the plants themselves. This constant cultivation is immensely beneficial not only to the potato, but to other crops. It admits the air into the ground, and allows the sun to exercise its influence upon the fresh soil that is constantly being brought into direct contact with it. It also helps to keep off any noxious insect pests, by exposing them to the birds; in short, the quantity and quality of the crop depends more upon the horse-hoe than we probably are aware of, and when it is considered at what little cost a man and horse may do an acre, potato growers should be most careful never to let the crop suffer in the least through want of it. If there is not a weed to be seen, and there has been no rain to make the ground stale since the previous hoeing, the improved crop will repay the little expense of this extra labour. If the season be dry, this constant stirring necessarily makes the soil more friable, which thus becomes not only the very thing for earthing up, but it greatly modifies the ill-effects of a protracted drought by helping to retain the moisture in the land. As the haulm increases in height and bulk, the cultivation between the rows must be narrowed, so as to prevent injury to the rootlets, which will be extending in every direction.

Thinning the Haulm.—The quantity of stems that each set throws up greatly determines the character of the crop. For example, when digging up it will be found that eight or ten stalks represent a host of small tubers, the majority of them fit for seed and chats only, with but few ware. On the other hand, where a root of potatoes throws up but two or three thick pieces of haulm, the tubes will run fewer and larger, and the proportion of seed and chats very small. Were it not for the time it would take to overhaul the seed at planting time and cut out the useless eyes, the thinning of the haulm later on would be unnecessary. At present, however, we must confine such preliminary operations to the limited culture practised in gardens and other small plots. As soon as the haulm is sufficiently forward to see the number and character of the stems from each root, women and big children should go over the field, row by row, and pull up all the stems that are not wanted. This should obviously be done as soon as possible before any tubers are formed upon them, which means a useless expenditure of energy by the set, and a certain waste of the manure. In pulling, the feet should be placed very near together on either side of the haulm, so that neither the surface of the ground nor the set underneath gets disturbed more than is necessary. To this end it is better to pull the stems singly, always leaving two or three of the stoutest and most healthy to carry the crop. When in the case of blight, all the haulm is pulled up to stop the disease descending to the tubers, unless the feet are put together or one hand kept tightly on the ground round each stem, of course many of the young potatoes will be pulled out of the ground hanging to it. A few, quick, intelligent hands will get over a good breadth of land in a day. If the object be to produce as much seed as possible from any particular sort, of course this thinning of the haulm need not be resorted to. We may remark here that at planting time the distance of the sets apart may be slightly regulated by the determination to thin, or not to thin, the haulm by-and-by.

Earthing.—Some growers do not adopt the

practice of earthing up their potatoes, believing that the yield is lessened by it, and their experiments would seem to confirm them in their belief. If they are correct, it seems evident their remarks can only apply to very light land wherein the rootlets would have nothing to obstruct their growth, nor the tubers anything to interfere with their proper development. We certainly should not look for a maximum yield of potatoes from sets put in stiff land 5 in. or 6 in. deep, having formed their tubers in soil that had been in a great measure unmoved during the whole period of their growth. Nor should we expect to find the shape and quality so good as those grown in fresh, loose soil sweetened by the sun. Many of the potatoes, too, would be formed near or upon the surface, and be more liable to the disease than those deeper in the ground, besides any actually in sight would become green and therefore worthless for eating.

The practice of drawing the earth to the rows is the better and more correct plan; but instead of throwing huge quantities of it against and over the haulm with the double boarded plough, half smothering it, it would often be better to partly earth the first time, and complete the operation later on. There are certain to be several plants which at the first earthing are not tall enough to receive the same quantity of mould as others, and which get well-nigh buried out of sight if the rows are done but once. Beyond the benefit these get by a second earthing, the whole crop receives a covering of fresh, pulverized, mellowed soil, which in its removal destroys myriads of seedlings just forming. Any weeds standing in the rows should, as far as possible, be removed before earthing and not buried alive.

The difference between the field and the garden cultivation of the potato consists more in the kind of the implements employed than in the nature of the work. Thus no better system can be adopted in the garden, or in small and irregular pieces of ground where horse labour cannot be used, than digging between the rows as deeply as possible with the three or four-tined fork, and laying the ground fine, of course being careful not to dig so close as to disturb the rootlets or the tubers. In extensive cultivation it obviously takes too long to adopt this plan, although in its results it is, no doubt, more effectual. So also as regards the use of the three-pronged hoe for earthing. This cannot be economically used by a grower with his hundred acres, although by its use each separate plant can have just the quantity of mould drawn to it that it seems to require. This and other special culture and attention which garden plots receive, account for the great degree of success often met with therein. We may state here that, as a general rule, those potatoes that produce an abundance of haulm should not be extensively grown in a garden, the space reserved therein being devoted more to those varieties that have but little top and occupy the ground as short a time as possible before ripening.

CHAPTER VI.

POTATO DISEASE.

AFTER the long and sad experience of this plague, many growers probably consider it ought to be catalogued with such hitherto incurable scourges as the mould in hops and rinderpest among cattle.

Every farmer or gardener who has had any experience of potato growing worth naming is aware of the devastation this disease sometimes causes. This was specially the case in the year 1879—a season that no one connected with agriculture will ever forget—whole acres, even, yielding practically no sound marketable tubers worth mentioning. In short the recurrence of the disease is so general, that it has become well-nigh the exception now to dig up any large breadth of ground in autumn, planted with potatoes, without finding them more or less affected with it, it being worse in wet than in dry seasons, damp, rainy weather being particularly favourable to its development.

Much has been and possibly much more will yet be written upon this subject, one writer advocating one theory and one another, with varied suggestions for its amelioration or its entire stamping out. We shall probably continue to hear, as we do now, that one of the virtues of some highly extolled new variety of potato is its ability to practically defy the attacks of blight, but each in its turn will be pretty certain to go the way of the others, until we succeed in applying a remedy that will prove effective whenever and wherever it is used.

First Indications of Disease.—We believe the fungus that appears on the foliage of the growing plant may be generally regarded as the first indication of the disease, and this finds its way down to the roots by following the haulm, or by the spores falling on to the ground and getting washed down to them; hence the affected tubers found when digging up. In a few instances possibly, although we are by no means satisfied on the point, the disease *may* commence in the tubers, and spread upwards to the haulm, owing somehow to the actual germs of the disease coming into contact with them. Mr. Carruthers, of the British Museum, whose opinion in the matter is entitled to much weight, assured us quite recently that he—like ourselves—had met with no case of the kind. His theory of the disease is that the spores may be present, yet still perfectly harmless, until the surrounding conditions of heat and moisture become such as to start them into growth, when, having penetrated through the outer covering of the foliage, the disease may be regarded as established, and, as is generally received, it spreads and is eventually communicated to the tubers below with more or less rapidity, according to the weather. Mr. J. L. Jensen, of Copenhagen, who some months ago issued a treatise upon "How to overcome the Potato Disease," adopts the theory that the spores fall from the diseased leaves, and are washed down to the tubers which thereby become blighted. The way in which Mr. Jensen combats this state of things seems very feasible, and has in his case, and not in his only, doubtless produced results calculated to elicit sufficient faith therein, to insure for it a good, honest trial, so soon as his proposed remedy becomes generally known. What this is will be found later on in this chapter.

The susceptibility of the plant to this plague is no doubt greatly affected by the conditions under which it grows, but the whole subject offers a wide field for scientific inquiry. Not only should we know more of the predisposing causes thereto, but also what will give that character to the foliage that will resist the formation of the fungus thereon or retard its spread after it has once struck the leaf; or if that be asking too much, now that the nature of the disease is understood, and the character of the resting spores so well known, we should be acquainted with something that will, upon being applied to the attacked plant, have the effect of destroying the vitality of the spores in the first stage of the disease, thus rendering the attack harmless.

We know wet weather greatly encourages the spread of the blight, and farmyard manure also tends probably in some degree to its development, inasmuch as it is calculated to induce a rankness of haulm favourable to its progress; but so great is the value of this manure in the production of the crop, and that which follows afterwards, that we are anxious to see the disease successfully dealt with without foregoing the use of the very best agent that we possess. Beyond this, the very large percentage of diseased tubers which have resulted from experiments tried with other manures and with no manures at all, furnishes us with an additional reason for not proscribing the use of farmyard manure in the culture of this vegetable.

Many whose hairs are now grey have a keen recollection of the first appearance of the potato blight. It is said to have been known in Australia three years before it came here, and some eleven years before that it existed in America. In Ireland, as everyone knows, its effects were felt much more seriously than in any part of the British Isles, reducing many of the inhabitants to the verge of starvation, resulting eventually in extensive emigration from that country to America. The circumstances connected with its first appearance have become a matter of history, but the completeness with which it did its work is so well expressed in a few words by an eye-witness that we give them here. He says that, as he passed from Cork to Dublin, in the last week of July, the plant was blooming in all the luxuriance of an abundant harvest; but returning a week later, he saw one wild waste of putrefying vegetation. Up to the present time, we are constantly reminded of this plague, although its ravages have not been so serious since then.

Evidence of Mr. Smith on the Disease.—Certain evidence given by Mr. Worthington G.

Smith, F.C.S., who has closely studied this subject, was appended to a Report of the Select Committee of the Commons upon the Potato; and, as it throws much light upon the character of the disease itself, and is otherwise full of interesting information, we give it for the benefit of the reader. Premising that the nature of the fungus which he alleges to be first in order of the potato disease, Peronospora infestans, a fungus which invariably accompanies the murrain, had probably been described to the Committee both by Mr. Dyer and Mr. Carruthers, he said: "A fact unaccountably lost sight of by many botanists is, that there is a second fungus parasite upon the potato plant, second in order with the Peronospora, and almost equally virulent with it. This second fungus is named Fusisporium solani. It commonly grows in company with the first open potatoes. Like the first, too, it disorganizes by contact, and it is almost, if not quite, as powerful in causing the utter destruction of the potato crop as the Peronospora itself. Both these fungi go to rest in an egg condition; the eggs, or 'resting spores,' as they are termed, of Peronospora, are capable of remaining in a hybernating state in the ground for a period of from one to three years before they show any signs of renewed life; whilst the resting spores of the Fusisporium seldom hybernate for a period longer than from three months to one year. It is a very easy matter to destroy the fruiting branches of both fungi whilst in a growing state, but the resting spores are able to resist climatic extremes of moisture, dryness, frost, and heat. The resting spores of both these fungi continue to hybernate whilst climatic conditions remain unfavourable to their active growth, but on the advent of a favourable amount of humidity and warmth they start into renewed life, and in the first instance grow on any material at hand, provided it is not caustic or corrosive.

"Microscopic fungi are commonly prepared for prolonged examination in glycerine, and nothing is more common than to see the spores of the potato fungus (and the spores belonging to many other fungi) growing in glycerine. The sudden onslaught, then, of the potato murrain each successive autumn, is caused by the advent of sufficient warmth and humidity to suit the germination of the resting spores. The resting spores are eggs of both the Peronospora and Fusisporium; they rest on and in the ground everywhere, especially in damp places and amongst decaying vegetable refuse. When these eggs at length burst, they generally protrude threads which carry seeds of spores, and these seeds are set free in uncountable millions. These seeds sail through the air, and such as fall upon potato-plants rapidly gain an entrance to the interior tissues of the host, and cause its corrosion and destruction. No doubt living resting spores, together with fungus spawn, are often planted with potatoes, and when this is the case the disease commences with the tuber and works upwards, whilst in the former case—*i.e.*, when the germination of the resting spores takes place upon the neighbouring ground—the leaves are the first part attacked from the air, and the disease works downwards to the tuber.

"Diseased potatoes when planted often produce perfectly sound crops, for it by no means follows as a rule that because a potato is merely discoloured and diseased, as potato growers say, it must invariably carry within itself healthy hybernating spawn, or hybernating spores, or seeds of the murrain capable of reproducing the disease. When potatoes once have the murrain decidedly upon them cure is perfectly hopeless. The potato plant is permeated by a poison hostile to and potent against its life, and no treatment can possibly renew the corroded and putrescent tissues of the potato plant. The position of the potato in a case like this is equally hopeless with that of a human subject under the last stage of blood poisoning or consumption. The above being my opinion of the hopelessness of cure, I will concisely confine my remarks to the answering of two more questions—viz., 1st. Why does the potato plant fall such an easy prey to murrain? 2nd. Is it possible to prevent or palliate the destructive virulence of each annual assault of the fungus?

"Why the Potato Succumbs to Murrain.— Why does the potato plant fall such an easy prey to the murrain? My answer to this is that, although there are many well-known instances of bad attacks of the murrain falling upon well-cultivated crops, yet, as a rule (and taking an average of the general mode of culture throughout the country), potatoes are badly stored, badly planted, badly cared for, and, moreover, carelessly and ignorantly thrown out of health. It must not be forgotten that the potato is not a hardy plant with us. It leads a somewhat unnatural life, under adverse conditions, and it requires nursing. When potatoes are stored, they require, as conditions of the first importance, both dryness and coolness, whilst, as a rule, potato-growers subject their potatoes to moisture and overheating. Stored potatoes are commonly piled in heaps during the entire winter, and in these death-heaps the potatoes get bruised, heated, and thrown completely out of condition. Stored potatoes are commonly in a hot-bed of disease. The potato-tuber, thus fermented and damaged, is now commonly cut into pieces, and the pieces, whilst still wet, are too frequently placed in the furrows of the ground in actual contact with rank dung and refuse, this material being saturated with spores and vermin of all sorts. The potato has by this time more or less lost its constitution, and the position in which it is planted too often adds to its troubles; for when potatoes are grown in marshy places and on flat alluvial plains, they require a different mode of culture from the same plants as grown in dry calcareous earth. As a rule, too, potato-growers crowd their plants too much together, and the potatoes are in as bad a plight for contracting disease as human beings and other animals are when constantly kept in overcrowded, ill-ventilated places.

"The potato murrain is not exclusively confined to the potato-plant, for it attacks with equal virulence (especially has this been the case in recent years) the tomato. This latter plant, like the potato, requires special care in cultivation; and where this care is not forthcoming, the whole crop is utterly lost. The murrain also attacks various wild plants in this country (principally members of the family to which the potato belongs); but these plants being healthy, hardy and natural to the soil and climate, throw off the murrain with ease, and rarely succumb. Records of facts of this class could be multiplied to an almost indefinite extent; hardy native and uncared-for subjects escape, whilst introduced subjects fall.

"For instance, there is a well-known disease of house-leeks, named Eudophyllum supervivi. This is one of the rarest possible occurrence on the hardy common house-leek of our roofs and gardens; but when the disease once gets amongst exotic species of sempervivum, it completely destroys every plant. It is the same with the hollyhock disease, Puccinea malvaccarum. The whole hardy single hollyhocks of cottage gardens throw off the disease with ease, whilst the tender, highly-cultivated garden varieties are utterly destroyed. Peaches, when grown on walls and exposed places, fall a prey to a disease named Ascomyces deformans, a disease almost unknown amongst peaches when carefully grown in fruit houses. Late fruiting garden peas are often completely destroyed by a fungus named Erysiphe martii, but this fungus has very slight effect upon the hardy wild peas.

"The following observations belong to a similar

class of facts. A racehorse may be as healthy as a waggon horse, and may be able to live as long a life; and a well tended spaniel as healthy as a Scottish shepherd dog; but one must be cared for in a different style from the other, if life and health are to be equally satisfactory in both. I conclude thereby, that the potato plant would not fall such an easy prey to the murrain if it received greater care in its general storage, planting, and cultivation. It now too often falls a prey to the infectious murrain, in the same way as the unclean and improperly fed human beings of populous districts fall before certain diseases, whilst clean, well-fed, and healthy individuals escape. Healthy, or apparently healthy, potato plants may occasionally succumb to the murrain, in the same way as a doctor may occasionally die from fever communicated by a patient.

"*Prevention and Palliation.*—The second and last question: Is it possible to prevent the destructive virulence of each annual assault of the fungus? is far more difficult of satisfactory answer. I, however, most certainly consider a good reduction of the amount of disease to be quite possible. The attacks cannot be mitigated by care, but a strong attempt might be made towards the prevention of the murrain. With a correct knowledge of the nature and cause, nearly every known disease can be prevented or palliated, especially when there is a specific poison in the case, as with the potato disease. As for stamping out the murrain, or isolating cultured experiments to an island in the sea, a short distance from the shore, any such attempt would be utterly futile. Spores are present everywhere, and can no doubt be carried through the air across a sea or ocean as readily as over a hedge. Spores everywhere sail with the wind, and at the same speed. Nothing is better known than the descent of spores, pollen, and other minute organisms, on to ships in mid-ocean. If potatoes were taken into an island in the middle of the South Pacific, or transported upwards miles into the air, or submerged for years in a river, they would yet be liable to contamination from the Peronospora, for the spores of the fungus are everywhere. The resting spores have been kept alive for three years simply in pure water, and have germinated after that time. In fact, the only way to satisfactorily see the ordinary spores germinate is in water.

"I have for many years been in the habit of constantly using the microscope, and I have found the spores of the potato fungus on the most diverse objects, and from the most diverse positions; showing that the spores must have been blown for long distances in every direction. Now, suppose the statement to be correct (which it is not) that the spores of the potato fungus are not carried far by the wind, are there no other means of dissemination at hand than disturbed air? Suppose a fox or hare runs through a field of infected plants, and then goes off to non-infected districts, he will carry tens of thousands of spores in his coat. Suppose a bird alights amongst infected potatoes; when that bird flies off he will carry tens of thousands of spores in his wings, and discharge them into the air as he sails over the country or the seas. The innumerable beetles, flies, moths, butterflies, and grubs found amongst potato plants, commonly swarm with spores. When a farmer goes into his infected fields he inhales the spores into his lungs, and when he eats his fruit from the walls of his kitchen garden he takes the spores into his stomach."

If we accept as an established fact the ubiquity of the spores of the fungus, we are driven to the conclusion that all who are practically engaged in the work of potato growing, must direct their attention towards fortifying the potato, as far as can be, against the attacks of this ever present enemy, so that its onslaught may be kept within the narrowest limits, and rendered as harmless as possible. In addition to this, until the time that we succeed in introducing new potatoes which are really disease resisting—if ever we be so fortunate—or attain the same end by the use of precautionary measures, we must have recourse to whatever treatment proves to be most effectual after the disease shows itself. In addition to this we must endeavour to grow such varieties as come to early maturity, but yet possess long keeping properties.

In Mr. Smith's reply to the query, "Why does the potato fall such an easy prey to this disease?" he justly reflects upon the unfair treatment to which it is usually subjected, which manifestly tends to weaken and render it more liable to succumb thereto.

We fear many potato growers could corroborate his remarks upon the manner of storing, &c.; still, anything which tends to bring into prominence these injudicious modes of dealing with the potato is of service, and suggests the propriety of employing a more rational system of treatment.

It is curious to note what a divergence of opinion exists upon the subject of the potato blight; thus one advances one reason as the cause, and some one else another. One maintains that it is occasioned by atmospheric influences, and the next that an insect is accountable for it. Many no doubt believe it to be contagious, whilst the author of a prize essay upon the subject says that he had three roots of shaws taken up in August, containing twelve sound and nine unsound tubers, which he placed on the bare ground, taking care that the diseased parts touched the sound ones. He then covered them with their own haulm and an old mat, examined them frequently, and lastly, in March, found the sound ones were all unblemished, whilst eight of the nine others were diseased all over, and one had only the upper eyes sound. All the conflicting views upon the subject are an evidence that the disease is shrouded in a certain amount of mystery, which we should like to see solved to the satisfaction of every one.

How to Grapple with the Disease.—In addition to the means at our disposal for restricting the ravages of the blight after it has made its appearance, which means have been more or less sanctioned by experience, we may doubtless adopt other measures of a preventive character at and previous to planting with very great benefit to the after crop, rendering the conditions as unfavourable as possible to the attack and spread of the disease. In general, those sorts should be grown which are not so liable as others to the disease.

Assuming or not assuming the existence of the spores upon the haulm and the ground around, we have abundant evidence that whilst one sort passes the season through unharmed, another variety close by becomes seriously attacked, it being the new kinds that for a while enjoy this immunity from disease.

This fact points to the wisdom of keeping up a continual supply of new varieties, from which those best suited to the table may be constantly selected. Healthy seed from stock comparatively free from blight the previous year should be chosen, in preference to that picked out of a crop that was much affected. Again, this seed should be stored during the winter in such bulk and where the temperature is so low as to prevent anything like dampness from perspiration, or premature germination. They should be planted before the shoots protrude far from the eyes and the potato feels in the least spongy; and when they are planted they should never be stinted for room, either in or between the rows. Further, they should not be placed in close contact with very rotten dung, and lastly well-drained land should be chosen with an open situation, in preference to low, ill-drained and confined fields, and particular care taken to keep the ground constantly moved during the whole period of their growth. Attention to these matters will bring its reward, since potatoes cared for in this way are certain to turn out very much better in almost every respect to those planted under opposite conditions. Should the blight attack them before they are quite ripe the haulm may be pulled up. This must be done carefully, the feet being kept near together, otherwise the potatoes will get pulled up with it, as was mentioned before. Cutting the haulm off we do not consider so effectual as pulling it up, particularly if the disease be very bad in it; but in one respect it is preferable, as it greatly helps the diggers by-and-by, indicating the situation of the roots, thus preventing them from inserting their fork into the midst of them, which they are liable to do when the haulm has all been removed previously.

Remedies Suggested.—All the various cures that have been suggested for the potato blight may be regarded as failures more or less, our own opinion being, that one of the best remedies known thus far, lies in the care of the seed and the good culture of the plant. We give one or two of such remedies in the words of the gentlemen who have seen such results from their application as to recommend their more extended trial. Thus a professional man has lately written as follows,—advocating the use of superphosphate for the purpose:—

"One year I planted a poor hungry piece of unclaimed common with potatoes. Not only was the land poor, but manure ran short and the tops, when they came, showed this very plainly. About a fortnight or three weeks before blossoming time, I sent in the plough and took away the crust at each side of the drill to within a few inches of the plant. In the furrow thus made I sowed bone superphosphate at the rate of three hundredweights to the acre, and then turned the mould thus enriched back to the plant. In about a fortnight, the poor, wiry looking tops assumed the deep green the plants usually have when first appearing above ground, and began at once to show signs of very vigorous life, thriving rapidly and throwing out fresh branches, till in about a month they completely covered the drills. About the time when the potato apples should begin to form, the disease attacked the rest of the field, but no disease ever appeared in this part, and the tops remained green till the autumn frosts came and cut them down, at which time, though there was an abundant crop of tubers, they were not fully ripe, but they were perfectly sound and remained so. This is strong evidence in support of the theory that the cause of the disease is a fall of temperature combined with heavy and continuous rain just when the plant has begun to be exhausted by the formation of tubers. As I was merely farming for amusement, I never followed up the experiment, nor planted potatoes afterwards, professional duties demanding all my attention; but I have no doubt whatever that this plan will baffle the disease, and I do not hesitate to recommend it to practical farmers. Of course care will have to be taken, and very great care, not to allow the plough to go too near the stems when taking away the land, and also not to give them so much manure at this time as will make them all tops and prevent them from ripening the tubers till the frosts come to cut them down. These points the practical farmer will soon learn to solve for himself. Let him try a small bit next year, or two or three small bits, making a difference in the treatment, and when he has satisfied himself which is the best, let him keep to that. Perhaps it will be wise to follow up the experiments for two or even three years before applying the method to a large crop. To my mind the plan commends itself for this reason—it preserves the whole plant, stem and tuber."

Mr. Jensen's theory with regard to the communication of the disease to the tubers is, as we said before, that the spores fall on to the ground and are washed down to them. Certain experiments having shown that the tubers principally affected are those lying nearest to the surface, seem to have confirmed him in this idea, inasmuch as he regards the upper layers of earth as retaining these spores, whilst as a consequence, the deeper lying tubers, comparatively speaking, escape the disease. This is of course in cases of partial blight. His observations further pointing out to him that the diseased potatoes were not only those near the surface of the ground, but were also chiefly found nearest to the stems, he concluded that the latter kept a passage open down to the tubers, besides conducting the rainwater by which the spores were carried thereto, making them peculiarly liable to be the first to become diseased. We will now quote from a letter of Mr. Jensen's in which he briefly describes the mode of treatment he has adopted with the results of the same; although we shall show later on the discovery is by no means one of recent date, inasmuch as similar experiments were made—and with success— many years ago. Mr. Jensen says:—" It is obvious that in fighting the disease the main object must be to prevent the spores from working their way through the earth to the tubers. My experiments have convinced me that this can be done to such a degree that even the most violent attacks of the disease may, as a rule, be almost neutralized. The means by which this may be effected are very simple. It is only necessary to throw up a high and sharp ridge of earth round the potato plants a little before the disease has appeared in the foliage, or at least at the very first appearance of it. The reasons why this operation should not take place at an earlier stage of the development of the plants has been explained in the treatise. The usual moulding hitherto practised in all countries is a *flat moulding*, by which the uppermost tubers are only covered by a layer of 1 or 2 inches of earth, but my protective system requires—after a preceding flat moulding—*a high and sharp moulding*, by which the upper surface of the uppermost tubers is covered with about 5 in. of earth. To effect this it is necessary that the ridge must be so high, that the top of it is 10 in. to

12 in. above the surface of the adjoining furrow, or ditch, whilst the ridge must be very broad at the bottom. My system also requires that the tops of the potatoes shall be moderately bent to one side, with a view to prevent the rainwater from running down the stems and thus carrying the spores to the tubers. By this contrivance, also, more spores will fall between than upon the ridges. In five places in Denmark last year (1881) the following results were obtained in eight experiments :—

	Diseased tubers by common flat-moulding.	Diseased tubers by high or protective moulding (tops bent)
Copenhagen	34·8	1·4
,,	6·1	2·0
Gl. Antvorskov	45·2	0·0
,,	44·5	0·3
Vallebo	7·7	1·1
Tvensbjerg	24·1	4·5
Sandal	18·8	0·3
,,	5·3	1·6
Averages	23·3	1·4

"From this Table it will be seen that in all the cases the disease has been considerably warded off by my protective system, and upon the whole it has been reduced from a very high degree to what may practically be termed a mere trace of it. The case of the experiment at Antvorskov especially deserves a more particular consideration. Seven rows were treated in the usual way, one was not moulded; eight other rows had been subjected to protective moulding. The results were as follows:—

An Early Variety.

For the flat-moulded and the unmoulded row.	For the high-moulded rows (tops bent).
29·2	0·5
22·6	0·0
45·2	0·0
38·1	0·0

A Late Variety.

24·6	0·0
64·3	0·3
44·8	0·0
57·6	0·0

"As in all the other experiments, the rows were growing side by side. The experimental plot was situated in a wet place at the base of a hill, and the rainfall was extremely high. The table shows that this violent attack had been so completely repulsed that there was hardly the slightest trace of diseased potatoes to be found in the protected rows. With regard to a series of controlling researches with the microscope I beg to refer to the treatise. The researches fully agree with the practical results of the field experiments, and prove that a very great reduction of the disease will *always* be the necessary consequence of protective moulding if this be carried out in due time, and in the manner described in the pamphlet.

"A strong warning must be expressed with regard

to the lifting of the potatoes. If this be done before the diseased foliage has quite withered it is impossible to escape without loss, because the tubers in the very act of lifting will be sprinkled by the millions and millions of spores hanging in the diseased leaves. For six days the tubers, which have been infected on that occasion, will appear to be quite sound, but on the seventh or eighth day (according to temperature), they will suddenly show the marks of disease. It is even not sufficient that the leaves are withered before the lifting; they must have been so for two or three weeks, otherwise many spores will be found capable of germinating, and thus be dangerous to the tubers when the latter are taken out of the ground Evidences to that effect will be found in the treatise. In the ground the tubers will be almost fully protected by high or protective moulding, and no progress of the disease, therefore, will take place as long as the tubers remain therein. To conclude, I beg to give the principal points in my protective system :—

"1. The ground must be thoroughly worked, so that the potatoes may be planted in friable earth, which affords a better means of protection than a lumpy soil.

"2. The potatoes should be planted (pretty early) at a distance between the rows of at least 28 in. or 30 in. A greater distance is not required by the system, but if closer it would impede the protective moulding.

"3. The first moulding must be flat, so that the formed ridge be broad on the top and only about

4 in. high. This moulding may be repeated if it is thought advisable.

"4. The protective moulding must be applied as soon as the disease-blotches make their appearance on the leaves of the haulm. If this has not occurred before wheat-harvest-time the moulding ought to be executed then, without waiting for the appearance of the disease blotches.

"5. The protective moulding is performed by throwing up from one side of the row of plants a high ridge with a broad base, and running to as sharp a point at the top as possible. The covering of earth thereby produced over the upper surface of the uppermost tubers must be about 5 in. to begin with; later, by the settling of the earth and by sliding down, it will, as a rule, preserve a thickness of about 4 in. Simultaneously with this moulding the potato-tops are gently bent over towards the opposite side of the row, so as to give the top at least a half-erect position.

"6. The flat and the protective moulding, where potatoes are only grown upon a small scale, may be done with a hand-hoe; on a larger scale these operations ought to be performed with a moulding-plough, the "Protector," which is constructed to meet the necessities of the described system.

"7. In order to prevent after-sickness, which may often be exceedingly great, the potatoes must not be lifted before about three weeks after the last leaves in the potato-field are withered.

"8. If the potato-tops are cut off and carried away,

which, for the sake of the quantity and quality of the crop, ought not to be done before the leaves, in the main, are withered, the lifting may, as it seems, without danger of after-sickness, take place about six days after such removal."

Dr. Lang, who wrote a prize essay upon "The Potato" in 1858, contended that the disease always originates in the leaf. Again, he noticed that those tubers which were well covered with earth enjoyed an immunity therefrom in a most remarkable degree. He says :—"It was determined to ascertain if possible what effect depth of soil might have on the produce of the set, and possibly on the disease. It was remembered that in 1847 and 1848, when the disease appeared to be greatly on the increase, and threatened to be, as it really was, most destructive, a man at Whilborough, on dry days, in order to save his potatoes, instead of digging them up, made the earth very fine, earthed the stalks up very high, and saved his crop most effectually." Further on Dr. Lang says:—"It was observed in taking up many acres of potatoes by many men that no potato covered with more than 3 inches of soil was ever diseased, and on repeating the experiment with very great care, I felt assured that no potato covered with 3 inches becomes diseased, and that their experience was correct. I have seen scores of bushels of potatoes dug, but I have never seen or heard of one diseased potato being found 4 inches under the surface of the ground, and too much stress cannot be laid on this fact that the disease is in exact ratio to the proximity of the tubers to the surface. To elucidate this, on September 18, 1857, three pits were made, 10 inches deep, and about the same in diameter. Three white kidney potatoes where placed horizontally in the bottom, and just covered with a little fine earth, then another layer similarly covered, and then a third layer, so that the whole consisted of three layers of potatoes, with just earth enough between to kept them from touching each other, and the uppermost layer about $2\frac{1}{2}$ inches under the surface. A few diseased leaves and stems were placed on the surface of pit No. 1, and then watered with half a small garden pan of water with a fine rose. Pit No. 2 was watered with the remaining water. Pit No. 3 had a large slate put upon it. September 28.—No. 1 pit had each of the upper three potatoes slightly affected. January 23, 1858.—No. 1, three upper potatoes quite rotten; No. 2, three upper much affected; No. 3, three upper not diseased. In all three pits both of the under layers were free from any taint."

Dr. Lang also proved that earthing high up very carefully whenever the first approach of disease occurred saved the crop to a very great extent, so that in this respect the experience of Mr. Jensen and himself agree. Dr. Lang's conclusions may be thus expressed in a few words :—" That the disease is of a fungoid nature, increased in virulency by atmospheric causes; that all manures are injurious save only lime and salt; that the earliest potatoes in ripening should be exclusively grown; that earthing up repeatedly with fine earth is the only effectual preventive of the disease." We take the following extract from the Eng. Soc. Trans. from a "Report on the Cultivation of Potatoes, with special reference to the Disease, 1874." Mr. John Frier, of Manor House, Chatteris, Isle of Ely, states: —" On looking back for nearly a period of thirty years over memoranda respecting the treatment of the potato crop, with special reference to the disease, I find only one set of experiments that have to any extent lessened the amount of loss. These experiments have all been based on the fact that covering up the haulm to within a few inches of the ends greatly hindered the progress of the blight, and ultimately it was found that the nearer to a horizontal position the haulm was placed in, the greater was the immunity from the disease. The first occasion on which the plan was tried was two or three years after the first appearance of the disease, when a large field was operated upon, the haulms being deeply moulded up on one side only, and the flattening down of the earth upon them was completed by hand labour. In that season this field remained green and growing up to Michael-mas, nearly every other field in the kingdom having been blighted the latter end of August. The plan was continued for a time, until the disease almost disappearing, it was given up."

A few years ago, however, it appears that a trial of it was again made. " A small portion of a field was 'laid down,' and the results were so satisfactory" (so says a gentleman in a weekly agricultural journal) " that last year nearly fifty acres were operated upon, and with great advantage. Careful observation brought to notice one important fact—viz., that those rows yielded the most and the finest tubers which were laid down towards the east, thus allowing the sloping side drill to be exposed to the afternoon and evening sun. A plough has now been made suitable for laying down all the haulms in one direction towards the east. This plough is about to be introduced to the public by Messrs. Howard, of Bedford. The theory as to the causes of the benefit secured by this process I leave to others to suggest. Whether it be that the descending spores of the fungus which produces the disease drop from the flattened stalks on to the earth, instead of descending to the root, and thus lose their power of mischief, or whether the 'laying down' checks for a time the too rapid and succulent growth of the tops, and thus prevents a weak growth of the tuber, it is difficult to decide; at any rate, a large saving is effected by the process." Then follow the results of a few experiments from plots set aside with this especial object: equal lengths of each plot were taken up, all having been cultivated alike and growing side by side:—

	Not moulded up.	
	Good.	Diseased.
4 rows of "King of Potatoes"	88 lbs.	123 lbs.
4 „ Regents	376 „	346 „
	464 „	469 „

	Haulm laid down.	
	Good.	Diseased.
4 rows of "King of Potatoes"	150 lbs.	46 lbs.
4 „ Regents	500 „	117 „
	650 „	163 „

From the foregoing we think we have adduced sufficient evidence to prove that the system of high earthing is of considerable value.

CHAPTER VII.

DIGGING AND MARKETING.

A CORRECT knowledge of when is the best time to dig is an important consideration in potato growing. Those who cultivate with the intention of clamping their produce and selling later on in the winter or spring, cannot do better than let the potatoes remain in the ground until they are perfectly matured, unless the blight gains such a powerful hold on them as to seriously threaten the crop, in which case they must be attended to promptly in order to save as many as possible. If, as we hope, Mr. Jensen's theory prove correct and his remedy effectual, we need not be much alarmed at the presence of the disease upon the foliage, but may give the tubers time to mature as long as there is vitality in the plant; but if his remedy will not stand the test which is claimed for it, the alternative is either to carefully pull up the haulm or dig the crop as speedily as can be.

If the season through has been favourable to the health of the potato, or if the plant is observed to ripen and die off naturally, of course no undue haste need be employed, and the crop can be raised, sorted, and clamped, or otherwise dealt with at the grower's convenience, but we recommend its being secured as soon as possible after maturity has taken place, and never left lying in the ground a week or a month longer than is absolutely necessary. No doubt the protracted harvests which follow our more backward summers of late, and the timely digging of potatoes are apt to conflict, and the latter operation gets shelved awhile, the fields becoming not seldom saturated with the autumn rains before the potatoes are housed away. In trying seasons we are often driven to do many things upon the farm as opportunity arises, and not just when we would prefer. Fine weather, however, should always be chosen for lifting root crops as well as for planting, as they come out so much cleaner and more easily, and the land escapes the ill-effects that continuous trampling has upon it in wet weather, especially if it be of a heavy binding nature.

The act of lifting potatoes is performed either with the fork or spud, or by horse power. The former is a capital tool for the purpose, and is destined probably to last as long as the plough itself, particularly in small and irregular fields and in gardens. Labourers accustomed to the work will make a pretty clean job with this implement, leaving but few behind, and piercing but few tubers, where there has been no necessity for pulling the haulm up previously. If, however, owing to the spread of the blight, it has been seen fit to arrest its progress by having it all removed, it obviously happens that sometimes the fork will come into too direct contact with the potatoes. The diggers should take a row each across the field, the outside man being slightly in advance of the one next him, and so on with the whole gang; whilst women or young people should pick up the potatoes, and we incline to the plan of allowing each to pick up a certain quality; thus one looks to the ware, another the seed, &c. If the number of hands following the diggers are carefully apportioned this plan will be found to work well, and the various classes are not so likely to get mixed as when one woman is perhaps clearing up everything as she goes, having three baskets to attend to.

A machine was brought out by Mr. Aspinall a few years ago which would, with a pair of horses, dig from $3\frac{1}{2}$ to $4\frac{1}{2}$ acres per day, leaving the potatoes on the top of the ground free from the haulm, just behind the machine, without injuring them, and where they could be easily picked up. On very light land two horses were scarcely needed. Where the ridging plough is used for turning out the produce, it should be set sufficiently deep to prevent its bruising the tubers. After those visible are all picked up, a gentle harrowing will bring most of the remaining ones to the surface, whilst it may be found worth the expense by-and-by of having a lad to follow the plough with a basket, and pick up any more that come to light when the land is being moved for the next crop. If, however, the potatoes have been harvested by the day, and reasonable care exercised, the ploughman's wife or daughter may be left to adjust this little matter for her own benefit. The plan of letting out the digging at so much per sack will, of course, need a corresponding amount of attention on the part of the grower to see that the work is done thoroughly in every respect.

The Marketing.—It is not so easy now as formerly to correctly estimate the probable prices which will rule our markets for various produce the season through. Competition having become so general and keen, and the means of transit so perfect, the whole tendency, as everyone knows, is to equalize prices everywhere, so that speculations for the rise must be ventured upon only after searching inquiry and observation. The prices potatoes may be making at digging-up time should always be regarded in connection with those which may or may not rule some time during the next six or eight months. When the expenses of twice handling, loading and unloading, clamping and unclamping, are all taken into consideration, if present prices offer a fair remuneration, and reliable information points to the existence of large yields generally, it would doubtless be to a grower's advantage to realize at digging-up time, and forego any further expense, instead of burying them all the winter, and running the risk of possibly worse prices in the spring. No hard-and-fast rules can, however, be laid down upon this point, and a figure it would be right to accept in one season, it would be wise to refuse another: 1s. 9d. a bushel at home in September for ware and seed, taken just as they come, might and does seem a somewhat insignificant price, but perhaps represents a larger or as large a net sum as would be forthcoming from the gross returns of the London markets some months later. In dealing with any such heavy ware as potatoes, savoys, rhubarb, &c., the question of freight is always one that demands almost our first consideration, it prohibiting their growth if the produce is to be carried very far to market.

The question to be decided regarding the disposal of early-grown potatoes differs somewhat from that in connection with later-grown ones. When perhaps Prolifies, Ashleaf, or in fact any early varieties are making four, five, or six shillings per bushel about Midsummer, the tubers in many fields that are rather more backward than others—possibly being not more than half or two-thirds grown—it becomes a nice point to settle (and it must be settled promptly) whether it is better to dig and market these comparatively small and unmatured tubers at the high prices then ruling, or defer the digging for a week or ten days just at this growing season, and so greatly increase the yield, but at the expense of a certain sharp fall in price. This is a question that often comes up for decision in the experience of those who grow for the early market, and whether we ought to pick our tiny green gooseberries or semi-ripened black currants and make 15s. or 20s. a bushel of them, or let them get properly developed and sell at possibly half that price presently, is just a point to be settled by the practical and experienced grower.

Everyone knows how carefully unripe potatoes should be handled, as their skin being unset it so easily rubs off, and then the sample is spoilt. They should be picked up in the baskets and shifting avoided as far as possible, the "toppers" being chosen and laid flat and even, and not such as to unduly or unfairly represent the bulk below. Some nice green haulm, with two or three hazel sticks or nut wands, form a fitting covering to the basket, or where pads are used, they may be covered similarly, but the lid must be tied down with a piece of thick string, and the net weight of the potatoes marked on a ticket attached to each, unless the salesman or buyer understands there is some exact weight, 1cwt. for instance, in each pad. The chats may sometimes be sold to a baker near for more money than they are worth for consumption by stock; but where they cannot be disposed of in that way, if free from disease, they may be stowed in some building, and a copperfull boiled as often as necessary, and fed to pigs and fowls to advantage, either mixed with their other food or given alone. Instead of giving diseased potatoes to any kind of stock, and carrying the affected haulm into the yard to find its way into the dung mixen later on, it would be better under such circumstances, to collect and burn both on the place, and in due course spread the ashes broadcast to be ploughed in.

CHAPTER VIII.

Clamping and Storing.—Having been fortunate enough to grow our potatoes, and having decided to stow them away for the winter, a piece of dry ground should be chosen for the clamp (supposing there be no building suitable or large enough to hold them) as conveniently near the homestead as possible. A trench should not be dug out for them, thus leaving the bottom of the clamp below the ground level, but, if anything, the actual base of the clamp is better resting on ground a little higher than that immediately surrounding it, or at any rate quite on the level, so as not to induce any surface water to drain towards it. Although digging out a long grave a spit or two deep actually helps to bury the potatoes, and the loose earth so removed comes in for healing the upper portion of the clamp, yet the plan mentioned above is preferable, and should be employed in similarly dealing with other roots also, especially where the character of the ground and the situation of the clamp are not such as one could wish.

As alluded to before, it is always best to choose fine weather for field operations with potatoes, and by no means clamp and then heal them in unless they are dry. Dug under these conditions, if the tubers roll out clean, and after being picked up are not too hastily carried away and emptied in the clamp, they may be considered as having fulfilled one condition essential to their proper keeping all the winter. Potatoes half hidden, with the soil clinging to them, should, whenever practicable, be left in the ground until the circumstances are more favourable, and never clamped in that state. If the disease be present, many unsound ones unavoidably escape detection, and lay the foundation for trouble in the heap, to be discovered when it is too late to repair the mischief. Should it happen, however, that the digging and storing must be done in unsuitable weather, the clamp, if of moderate size, should be temporarily protected with some improvised covering while the weather is actually wet, the same being removed when it clears up. In due course the potatoes may be covered with a thick layer of straw, and the earth dug from near the clamp and laid some 6 inches or upwards thick all over it, thicker on the north or eastern side as the case may be; remembering always that while frost must be kept away from the potatoes, burying them too deeply before this takes place tends to promote untimely sprouting. As the work proceeds the earth should be beaten down firmly and smoothly, so as to carry off the rain, whilst small tufts of twisted straw should be left protruding through the mould, at every few feet along the ridge, for ventilation, the soil being arranged securely around them. As an additional protection against frost, the clamps in Kent are sometimes covered over with hop bines tied up into bundles. Potatoes, through going so much closer together than wurzel or swedes, require to be stored in a much smaller bulk, about a yard or so at the base of the clamp being a fair width, and the sides carried up about steep enough to lay the earth on without much difficulty. Of course, where several sorts are stored in one long range, the position of each must be distinctly marked, and so arranged that it can be got at with a minimum of trouble when wanted. The great point to be aimed at in successful clamping or other storing is to make the heap of such solidity as shall admit of its duly casting off any vapour generated therein, and this must be more carefully determined in proportion to the state of the temperature at the time of healing the clamp in, and the condition of the roots as regards being dry and fully ripe. They must not be expected to keep long and well where these points are overlooked.

Root Houses and Cellars.—When any one is fortunate enough to have a good root house at his disposal, such as is used in America, a kind of cellar made in a hill-side or elsewhere near the premises, with either clay or brick walls as the case requires, much labour and expense are saved. The bottom of hop kilns, too, in districts where they abound, may be utilized for winter storage; but when the digging is going on before the hop season is over, the temporary housing of the potatoes in a barn or elsewhere presents an opportunity for their drying, and for detecting any diseased ones when shifting them a few weeks afterwards. If disease be present, it is always better not to be too hasty in covering them in, potatoes apparently sound when stored having turned out terribly bad. Experiments have been made with lime, which has proved a valuable agent in warding off disease. Placed on the bottom of a clamp or otherwise, and covered so as not to come into actual contact with the potatoes, it has yielded very satisfactory results. Where but few comparatively have to be stored for home consumption or otherwise, an hour or two can be often found for overhauling one's stock, so that when they are finally put by they may be reckoned quite sound. Kilns are very different to cellars, owing to the draughts from the dome overhead, and the ventilators round the sides. These latter must of course be properly closed and secured, and the potatoes well protected with straw, whilst the floor above must also be covered to exclude the cold air.

The advantages an ordinary house cellar has over these is readily seen, the temperature therein being uniform and comparatively high; and potatoes put into the American flour and apple barrels, and stood therein out of the light, will keep good as long as they are wanted, if as the spring approaches they are overhauled and the sprouts rubbed off. This last remark, however, applies to potatoes for home consumption rather than to those set apart for seed, which by that time should be moved with a view of planting, unless their quarters have been too warm and premature sprouting in the winter promoted thereby. We have seen the Early Rose in a friend's cellar in London having shoots well-nigh half an inch long by the middle of December. It is evidently unwise, when avoidable, to subject any potatoes, whether seed or otherwise, to such treatment, for as any one knows who has kept potatoes, the quality of the ware for eating is adversely affected in proportion as the substance is carried off in the sprouts, and the seed likewise weakened for planting.

A large grower of potatoes in New York State has published in the *American Cultivator* his system of storing in the winter, a reproduction of which may be read with interest whilst treating of this branch of potato culture. " The potatoes are put in middling tight bins, of a capacity of from 50 to 500 bushels each, and, if need be, 3 ft. or 4 ft. deep in the heap. As soon as thus stored they are covered with a course of straw, which prevents the top specimens from turning green, and besides absorbs or aids in removing the moisture generated by the potatoes. A few weeks later, or before winter sets in, draw a good load of earth—a light sandy loam is best—and cover the straw 3 in. or 4 in. deep, which places the tubers in nearly the same condition as buried or pitted potatoes. This operation is much more easily performed than pitting in the field, for a single load of earth is sufficient to pit over a bin of from 200 to 300 bushels.

"There are several advantages in this system of management. First, the potatoes are well housed, and in such a location that they can be easily looked after at any time. Security against frost is maintained even if the cellar is cold. If wanted at any time for market or other purposes they are accessible on short notice. The fresh and crisp quality so much desired in potatoes is retained in as high a degree as those specimens stored in pits. By this method of storage the percentage of shrinkage is far less than by the open-bin method. In fact, I find in my experience that I save enough in weight alone, on the lots I sell, to pay me well for the extra expense of earthing them over. I recommend keeping the storage cellar quite cool. Potatoes stored by this plan do not sprout so early in the spring as those kept open in the cellar, but they should be uncovered early, since the sprouts will grow very rapidly on them after commencing. Potatoes thus stored retain their good quality as well as those in pits, while the grower secures the use of his cellar as a storage place." We gather from this that these bins stand in a cellar, probably one of the kind alluded to above; their size, and the thickness of the wood used, depend of course upon the quantity of potatoes they are to hold.

An Irish journal in a recent issue has the following most appropriate remarks upon this subject of "Wintering Potatoes." It says:—"Apart from actually rotting, there is nothing so injurious to potatoes in winter as starting into growth, and it is this that must be guarded against now and afterwards. Champions, Rocks, Queens, and Magnum Bonums are always late in beginning to grow, but early and mid-season sorts are ever ready to grow on the slightest excitement. The larger the heaps the more their contents seem inclined to grow, and for various reasons it is best if potatoes can be spread pretty well out. By this I do not mean that they should be in single layers, but a mass of them a foot or so in depth is deep enough. In high hillocks or ridges, potatoes for table lose much of their flavour, and those intended for seed are not benefited thereby. Seed potatoes and those for eating are better kept separate, and all who wish to care for them both properly, generally try to treat them differently. Potatoes for eating should be kept well in the dark now, as when exposed to light for any length of time they soon become green and bitter. This takes place as quickly now as it would have done when they were newly lifted, and although very little light may be admitted to them, this may be sufficient to taint them. When potatoes are in houses or sheds a continuance of wet weather may make the place in which they are stored very damp, and to dry up this it may be necessary to let air and light in, but openings to do this should only be made on a dry day, or, better still, when dry at night. In some places, however, they may be stored where the doors or the windows have to be opened frequently, and then sufficient straw or some other covering should be thrown over them to kept the light from them. Eating potatoes which have been put in pits and covered with soil may be looked into occasionally, and when it is seen they are all right in one part further search for failures need not be made, but they should not be left too long without knowing how they are keeping, or much loss may occur. If there is no decay, sometimes they may be sprouting, and therefore will require attention. Seed potatoes may be kept in any light place, as it does not matter how green they become, but they must not be allowed to sprout until just before planting time."

The whole system of storing is determined greatly by the quantity of potatoes to be dealt with; and while those who grow but few have little difficulty in finding a place suited to them through the winter, others differently circumstanced must adopt some such means of taking care of them as have been described above. The following is given as one way of preserving a limited quantity: "Have shallow boxes of a size that are handy to lift about, in which the potatoes should be set carefully up on end and close together, so as to wedge and support each other in their places; and in this manner they may be stored till planting time, and carried off to the ground where they are to be planted without any further handling. The cooler and more airy the situation in which they are placed the better; and therefore, if in sheds, door and windows should be thrown open during the daytime whenever the weather is favourable. Where space is limited, and boxes are placed one on the other, it is very important that plenty of space be left between them; this may be secured by blocks of wood 3 in. or so thick laid at each corner of the boxes, or by using pieces of brick in the same position." Cooking potatoes may be put into bins, but where their backs are formed by outer walls, boards should be put up, with something between, sawdust for instance, to keep out the frost. Turning potatoes may be done with a shovel, whilst sorting is much more quickly and easily done by means of a riddle or sieve, with properly sized meshes. The meshes may be square, and a couple of hands, one to work the sieve and the other (who may be a mere youth) to keep filling, will sort a great many in a short time.

Considerable quantities of seed may be stored in any room secure from frost and severe draughts if several rows of wide shelving be run up round the walls and the potatoes placed thereon. They need only to be made of rough wood, and strong enough to carry their freight of say a foot or less thick, which may then be very easily labelled, and kept from getting mixed with any other sorts. Besides this, being always under one's eye, their sprouting can be promoted or retarded at the owner's pleasure. The simple act of shifting and turning potatoes is very beneficial, as tending to prevent them prematurely shooting, and in some instances it would not be labour lost to shift a whole clamp about the middle of February in suitable weather, when, if not previously done, the seed and ware might be stowed away again separately for a few weeks — being heaped less thickly—till wanted.

CHAPTER IX.

RAISING SEEDLING POTATOES.

WHILST perhaps it can be scarcely expected that farmers will as a rule devote much time and attention to the raising of new varieties, it is an interesting and most useful study nevertheless. We have hinted before that the continual raising of new sorts seems to be a wise feature in potato culture, when we have to do battle with the dread disease from year to year. Every one who, as the result of patience and close observation, from time to time introduces to the public some new potato, possessing hardiness of constitution, good table qualities, or a capacity to resist in a great degree the attacks of blight if only for a few years, renders a real service to the public; and whilst for the present at any rate, the generality of our farmers have all their time, energy, and resources taxed to the utmost in order to simply maintain a position of solvency, the following remarks upon this subject will doubtless be useful to others who have more time and opportunity at their disposal for prosecuting this study.

The following is from a paper read recently by a successful Scotch propagator, who says:—

"New varieties are thus propagated:—Every seed yields a new sort, and some exhibit so decided a tendency to sport or change that almost every tuber is distinct from the other. This is a constant source of disappointment, for it not unfrequently happens that those plants which to all appearance are the finest turn out comparatively worthless, yielding in some instances not so much as one in a hundred that will repay the expense and labour required to bring it to maturity. The potatoes will be in a condition for eating in their third year, and at this period of their growth a very fair estimate of their quality may be formed; but it will take from four to five years, and sometimes a longer period, to bring them to their best state. If an ordinary amount of care be exercised, little difficulty will be experienced in obtaining a fairly good variety, or a potato with several good points; but it is by no means an easy matter to produce an article with all the qualifications required to ensure universal commendation. It must crop well, give uniformly large tubers of good quality, and be possessed of sufficient vigour to resist successfully the attacks of the blight. The last quality is the greatest desideratum, and the prize for which all growers have struggled, though very few have succeeded in going so far. Even when success is most complete to all appearance, it is found that the vigour which enables it to repel the ravages of disease gradually subsides, and after a few years disappears entirely.

"In the Report of the Royal Commission of Inquiry on the subject it is set forth that from the evidence it must be concluded no variety of potato cultivated from the tuber could maintain sufficient vigour to resist blight for many years in succession, and that if the potato were to be maintained as a profitable field crop, or as a useful article of food, more attention must of necessity be given to the propagation of new varieties from seed. The collection of the plums or seed apples from which to produce the tubers is a delicate process, and requires great skill and care. Both the very early and the very late maturing ones should be avoided, and the intermediate—such as are well matured at the time of collecting, and the greatest possible number of flowers fructified—only selected. When the plums are gathered they should be well dried, after which the seeds are removed, and stored in a dry, airy place.

Sowing the Seeds.—"About the end of March take a small box and put about 2 in. of dry moss into the bottom to carry off excessive moisture, and fill up with a mixture of rotted turf-mould, very fine sand, and leaf-mould in equal parts, well mixed and sifted. Sow the seeds on the surface, and cover thinly with fine mould. A little bottom-heat will be required until the seeds are well germinated, after which the box should be kept as near to the glass as possible. Care should be taken to avoid frost, and the seedlings should be thinned early to prevent their being drawn up and becoming spindly in habit. If sufficiently strong they may be planted out during the first or second week of June, reserving a few to fill up vacancies should any occur. After being planted out they require to be treated like any other bedded-out plants; keep clean, and frequently stir the surface to keep it loose and open. Take notes of any distinctive features in any of the plants, or of anything you would like to remember, and compare at a future date. Only those that seem better than ordinary should be entered in the register the first year." The grower then proceeds to give the result of some observations made by himself. One plant yielded 109 tubers, which weighed $1\frac{1}{2}$ lb., another 92 tubers and a third 84, which weighed upwards of 30 oz. Several others produced from 60 to 80 tubers, the weight of tubers, foliage, and roots in the case of one plant reaching $8\frac{1}{2}$ lb.

"The second year's crop was planted in rows of 15 ft. in length and 26 in. in breadth, with fourteen plants in each row, or little more than 1 ft. for each. At the end of the second year the plants require increased attention. They must be all numbered and entered in a note-book, with the number of the row in which they are growing, and it will be well to reserve a large space for remarks to be filled in as they grow up, such as the date of their appearance above the soil, whether robust or weakly, anything about their habits or character, colour of flower, general form, size, and colour of leaf, &c. When lifting, all the good tubers should be counted and weighed, and put in separate parcels, with the book-number attached. Reject the bad kinds. From every plant of only an ordinary character one of the best-shaped tubers should be selected, and the collection stored, and marked as mixed. These lose their descriptive number, and do not claim much attention the following season. The potatoes of the third year are treated in a similar manner. Those previously selected as good still retain their numbers, and are planted in the third year, devoting most space to the more promising plants. The greatest importance is attached to the form of the tuber, and large specimens are discarded in consequence of not being so shapely as the small. There is in this and the following stage a disposition to sport, and this requires great watchfulness. It is a great recommendation to any variety that it turns out true in form."

The *Rural New Yorker* has a very interesting and clearly written article upon seedling potatoes, which any one wishing to know more about practically would do well to study, and carry out the advice contained therein. It says:—

"It doesn't require a very long stretch of imagination to realize the fact how very slow and enterprising most become in supplying the farm with good and suitable seeds. Take the potato, and note carefully what might be done to promote its cultivation by a well-sustained effort in raising new varieties from seedlings. There is nothing comparatively easier to obtain than the potato apple or ball, or to provide than a sunny room or greenhouse, in which to sow the seeds in the autumn. If not, by the aid of a flower-pot or so and the sunny window, we may, from seed, produce tubers large enough for the table in two seasons. In fact, the seed may be sown in prepared plots out-of-doors in early spring, and, if well attended to, they will produce tubers which the next year will grow as large as the smallest of what are called marketable potatoes. To begin, let us gather the

"Seed balls, Apples, or by whatever name one chooses to call them, from the potato vines as soon as they begin to die. These may be kept until they begin to wither or rot, when the flesh has perished from the seed, and the latter dried and preserved the same as any other seeds, until sowing time arrives. The seed ball of a potato is the proper fruit, as the tomato is the fruit of the tomato plant. The tuber of a potato is merely a swollen underground stem, quite distinct from the roots. Indeed, tubers often form above ground in the axils of the green stems, as no doubt all of our readers have had occasion to notice. The so-called 'eyes' of a potato tuber are buds, which, as we also know, often push and form stems and leaves, feeding upon the decomposing flesh of the tuber itself. Potatoes may be, and are, grown from these stems, and in this way large quantities may be raised from a single tuber by pulling off the shoots and planting them as they grow. But this is a branch of the subject which need not be treated here. In times gone by potato plants fruited plentifully, and potato apples could be procured in unlimited quantities. It is different now.

"Many kinds do not fruit—some of them do not even bloom. Two years ago we raised sixty-two different varieties, and were unable either to procure any pollen for the purpose of crossing or a single seed ball. The past season, of fifty different kinds, ten only bore seed balls. When it is considered that potatoes have been bred and cultivated for the tubers alone, it is not surprising, perhaps, that the plants should incline to fruit less and less every year. Some say that the yield of potatoes fifty years ago was greater than now, and that therefore the potato is less productive now than then. This while perhaps true in fact, is no doubt an erroneous view as to the cause. If our ancestors had had our present varieties, they would probably have produced very much larger crops. The buds or eyes of potatoes sometimes vary, producing potatoes that differ in quality, in colour, or in time of maturing. Thus we have the Late Rose, Beauty of Hebron, &c., from Early Rose and Beauty of Hebron. But potatoes never 'mix in the hill' from contact, as some suppose. We can produce new varieties at will from the seed. Readers of this paper have been reminded during the past season to save seed balls, so that they might raise their own seedlings from year to year, instead of importing potatoes for seed or purchasing at exorbitant prices. That this has not been the rule, instead of the rare exception, is a fact difficult to explain—unless it is that the supposed difficulty of raising seedlings has stood in the way. Now we proceed to show that there is no trouble about it.

"**Selection of Seeds.**—It seems hardly necessary to advise that balls from the best varieties should alone be saved—the best yielders, the best in quality, in shape; the best keepers, and those which are least liable to disease of any kind. If our own potato vines produce no balls, probably they may be found in our neighbour's fields or patches. If they, too, fail, we may write to friends in other localities, or we may purchase them from seedsmen. We will suppose that our readers have neither greenhouses nor plant frames of any kind. We should next require a sunny window facing the east or south, or, better, south-east, and a room in which the temperature never falls below 35°. Provide well-drained pots filled with mellow garden soil. Press the soil firmly with the bottom of another flower pot. Then sow the seeds evenly half an inch apart and cover with one-eighth of an inch of soil, and again press the soil—this time lightly. Place these pots in pans or buckets of water so that the water comes up outside the pots nearly as high as the surface of the soil, and leave them until the surface soil begins to show it is wet. Remove them to the sunny window and cover each with glass. So treated they will need no more water until germination takes place, which will be in about a week or ten days. The glasses may be removed as soon as most of the seeds have sprouted. It is better, however, to remove the glass gradually, first by raising it an eighth of an inch, then a quarter, and finally lifting it off entirely. We prefer this method of supplying water to surface watering for several reasons, chief among which is that the soil is not washed off the seed. We should advise that the seeds be not sown until early in March. The little plants will then be large enough to transplant to little pots (say, 3 inches in diameter) by April. A pocket-knife blade is as good as anything for the purpose of 'pricking out' the plants, two or three of which may be planted in a 2½-inch pot.

"By April 20 many leaves will be found, while the plants will have reached the average height of 4 inches—some strong, some puny. The one thing now to be borne in mind is that these seedlings do not receive a check from over or insufficient watering, from too much or too little heat, or from any other cause, otherwise the swelling stems or little tubers will cease to grow, or they will make a second growth. As soon as all danger of frost is over, we may now transplant our seedling vines to a warm, well prepared plot. Dig little holes with a trowel, 1 foot apart in drills 3 feet apart, and thump the balls of earth, which will be held firmly together by the fibrous roots of the plants, out of the pots and set them firmly in these holes. Thereafter their treatment will be the same as potato plants from eyes. .The variety of which we selected seed last season was the English Magnum Bonum, as the flavour of this potato is good, and it is highly prized for its productiveness. Some of our vines from this seed died in August, while some of the vines were still green when the little crop was harvested—viz., September 30. Our plot consisted of three drills 3 feet apart and 8 feet long, the plants a foot apart in the drills.

"The Seedlings.—We harvested, of large and small, 600 potatoes, running from the size of a large pea to that of a hen's egg. Those smaller than a large pea were not gathered. The skins of all were white. The vines were cultivated flat, though, when the vines begin to die and to expose some of the tubers which have grown out of the ground or from which the soil has been washed by rain, it is better to cover them somewhat with soil. Otherwise they will 'green.' Our instructions have been for those who have no glass structures. Those who have greenhouses in which the temperature can be regulated at all times, may begin as early in the winter as they are pleased to do so. As the smaller pots become filled with roots, they should be thumped out into larger ones and supplied with more soil. We have placed our seedling potatoes in a basket of dry sand, supposing this to be the safest method of preserving them. Next spring we shall plant the small tubers whole, and cut in halves the larger ones, and from them we shall look for a fair proportion of saleable potatoes as to size. The tubers will, of course, vary as to shape, depth of eyes, colour of skin, earliness, &c., and a year or so further will be required to separate them according to such differences."

Messrs. Bliss and Sons, of America, in their catalogue, give the following advice upon the subject of raising seedlings :—

"Save any well-ripened seed-balls from a good variety, and plant in early spring, in well-drained boxes of sandy loam. Sow the seed on the surface, and sift fine soil over them to the depth of $\frac{1}{4}$ to $\frac{1}{2}$ an inch; water sparingly, and when the seedlings are 3 inches high, remove them from the seed box without disturbing the earth around them more than is necessary, and plant in more roomy quarters. Many successful growers, however, prefer sowing the seed in open ground, when a partially shaded spot may be selected, and the seeds may be sown in drills about 10 inches apart, and covered with $\frac{1}{2}$ inch of soil. When the plants are strong enough, transplant in rows 3 feet apart, 2 feet in the rows, and keep down the weeds until the tubers ripen. Some few strong growing varieties, will form tubers weighing from 6 to 8 ounces the first year. As a general rule they will be about the size of a walnut. Store the tubers carefully until the next season, keeping them as cool as may be without freezing, when they may be planted in the same manner as any mature potato. It usually takes three years to ascertain the true value of a seedling, and if a person is favoured by finding one really good variety among the many seedlings, he may feel well repaid for his time and trouble. Many new varieties are raised by hybridization, which is a more difficult method, although it generally secures a greater number of good varieties. The manner of procedure is as follows: Remove all flowers excepting those you wish to hybridize, then with a pair of sharp scissors remove all the anthers from the stamens in the flowers to be impregnated, just before they commence to discharge their pollen. When the flowers are dry, shake the flower containing the stamens of the variety which you wish to cross with it, being careful to do it when they are ready to discharge their pollen. Fit a piece of fine netting over the impregnated flower, to prevent the bee and other insects from leaving the pollen of other varieties upon the exposed pistil. The covering may be removed after two or three days. Do not disturb them again until the seed-ball has ripened, when the treatment as given in the first part of this article may be applied. Instances have been known, though rare, where one potato would produce two distinct sorts from its different buds or eyes. The White Peachblow, for example, has been found growing on the same stalk with the Jersey Peachblow. As so much interest is now excited in the growth and propagation of new seedlings, and many of the new varieties command such high prices—it behoves our farmers and amateur gardeners to avail themselves of the latest and, by actual tests, the best method of producing new varieties."

CHAPTER X.

POTATO SELECTION.

In our opening chapter we enumerated many varieties of potatoes that offer a fair field for choice to any one contemplating their culture, whether for exhibition, market, or more particularly for home use. As has been previously observed, the quality of a potato is affected by conditions of soil, and doubtless by locality also, so that it is imprudent to recommend in a too dogmatic spirit the universal culture of any special varieties to the exclusion of all others, because they happen to do well in one's own neighbourhood. Again, a prolific, hardy, marketable, and table variety, if it be found to thrive fairly well in any particular district, should certainly not be too hastily supplanted by one comparatively little, if at all, known in the locality. The introduction of the latter should be of a tentative nature at the outset, and a few seasons will decide its fate. Some old standard kinds are generally known and cultivated, and many others exist, probably, as well suited to the purpose. A correspondent writes upon the subject of "Potato Selection" thus:—

"There are doubtless many practical men and even more amateurs who would welcome a discriminating, yet concise, list of the sorts of potatoes most suitable to our climate. It may be thought that the descriptive lists issued by specialists and the nursery trade generally are sufficient for all practical purposes, but too frequently they are misleading, and, therefore, sorts are grown which would not be were their qualities better known. The trade does not trouble itself to any great extent to ascertain by actual trial in a variety of soils and localities, and by the crucial test of cooking at different times of the year, those that best deserve extended cultivation. A good tuber should have: 1st, good quality—*i.e.*, it should not be wet, or too waxy, but mealy and dry; 2nd, flavour, an agreeable nutty one being generally liked; 3rd, cropping capabilities; 4th, form, the outline pleasing, free from unsightly knobs and deeply sunken eyes. Colour is not of much consequence when not imparted to the flesh. It should also be stated at which time of the year the kind is at its best for table use.

"It seems a tolerably well ascertained fact that some kinds of the potato have in the course of years actually deteriorated. They do not always bear out what was once reported of them. The older sorts of kidney possessing that first of all qualification of a garden potato, flavour, were all of them only very moderate bearers, at least if adjudged by the productiveness of the later American and English kinds, and it was in the nature of things, that they should make way for the more abundant food producers of to-day. But these new sorts, although fine in form are deficient in flavour, and it is a matter of fact that some of the old-fashioned ugly tubers, with deep eyes, now relegated to the garden of the cottager, stand far higher, as regards flavour, than some of the much-vaunted exhibition sorts. Hybridizers should therefore look to this. It would also be gratifying to know which of the more recent varieties produce the best results as regards all points, in all soils." But, after all, a little perseverance with new sorts, in testing their qualities and suitability for any particular locality, is probably the best practice to adopt. A grower for the market, who *must* keep pace with the times, or a gardener who likes to have anything fresh and good in his own garden, can soon ascertain for himself what kinds he may safely plant in quantity, if from time to time he procures a little seed of some half a dozen of the latest and most approved kinds, and gives them all a trial. By this means old sorts, as fast as they go out of cultivation, can be easily replaced by something good. If the soil of some far off county will not give that nutty flavour to the potato that the stiff clay loam found in Middlesex is claimed to do, perhaps in some other respects it will produce a better potato. For securing flavour and mealiness in the tubers, one grower recommends that phosphatic manure should be used in preference to ammoniacal, and he enumerates a few potatoes that do well with him in the county named above. Thus, Rector of Woodstock, Early Market, Radstock Beauty, Champion, and Bedfort Prolific, are particularly good; of later varieties Reading Hero, Schoolmaster, and Champion, are first-rate. Of kidneys, he regards the Ashleaf as perhaps our best-flavoured early kind, and adds to it Mona's Pride, Covent Garden, Perfection, Edgcote Seedling, Advance, Woodstock Kidney, and Bountiful (small, but excellent in quality); and for its disease-resisting powers, Magnum Bonum. Of the newer kinds of well-proved table quality, whilst being large croppers and handsome at the same time, he recommends Cosmopolitan, White Kidney, Prizetaker, Red Kidney, and Reading Russet.

CHAPTER XI.

Forcing Potatoes.—There are some who think that, because they have only a garden frame or a few old lights to spare, it is useless attempting to force potatoes, but if they have these appliances, and a little stable manure or fresh gathered leaves wherewith to impart the necessary bottom-heat, they are as well circumstanced for forcing potatoes as they need desire to be. In order, however, to economize the fermenting material as much as possible, and impart a regular, genial warmth to the soil, the best plan is to get some rough hedge prunings, a few faggots, branches of trees, or any rubbish that will lie loose and hollow enough to allow heat to pass freely amongst it. This collected, the next thing is to measure out a piece of ground a trifle larger than the frame, on which to build a foundation with such of the above-named gatherings as are available to set it on. If this be done to the height of about 1 foot or 18 inches, fresh fermenting material can be added at any time, and a much less quantity suffices than if the bed were built up solid in the ordinary way. Not only is this the case, but it often occurs with hot beds, after they get a weight of earth placed on them, that the heat rapidly declines and soon ceases altogether, and that at a time when most wanted; whereas if formed with a base of rough stuff, a lining can be added at pleasure, by which means a uniform temperature may be maintained as long as the crop requires its assistance. Another advantage in making forcing beds up in this way is that the manure requires no previous preparing by being turned to sweeten it, which is a great thing, considering the amount of labour such work involves, and that at a season when there is much else to be done. With a frame so made up, a barrow-load or two of fresh manure or leaves may be thrown around it at any time, and the waning heat thus revived and kept steady on, which could not be done were the bed close and solid, as then it is impossible to drive it in.

In selecting a site for the frame, a sheltered, sunny spot should be chosen, so as to get as much benefit from the solar rays as possible, and prevent cold, cutting winds, that generally prevail during February and March, from blowing the heat out. To stop the soil from running amongst the faggots or whatever material is used for the foundation, 6 inches or so of short litter or leaves should be scattered, and on this the mould for planting the potatoes. The most suitable for this purpose is such as is of a light, rich, sandy nature, on which the potatoes will not only produce a great number of tubers, but they will all come with bright, clear skins, and this adds greatly to their appearance and quality when cooked. A soil containing lime rubbish or fresh crude manure is sure to spoil them by rendering them scabby, or causing warty excrescences or other deformities, and should therefore be avoided where fine quality is aimed at.

To make the most of the room without unduly crowding, the tubers may be planted in rows 1 foot apart, and about 8 inches from each other, which affords ample space for the tops if they are kept sturdy and strong by giving plenty of air. Those who happen to have the convenience of a small forcing-house or other warm place may considerably forward the sets by placing them in sifted leaf-soil in boxes to give them a start, and this is a capital plan, as a great many may be packed in a small compass and time saved while the bed and frame are being got ready. Many plant in small pots to commence, but they are in no way better than a shallow box, and take much more room and time to handle, as when laid in the latter they can be quickly transfered without the least injury. When moving some about the end of January that have been so treated, they will shift with masses of roots and a tuft of leaf-soil as big as one's fist, which will be a great help to them till they make further progress, and till they require something more substantial on which to lay hold. In most gardens it is the practice to make up a hot-bed to sow seeds on, but the same thing may be done in a potato frame, and valuable space thereby economized by making it serve the double purpose. Such things as early celery, cauliflowers, lettuce, and Brussel sprouts may all be raised in this way, and pricked out elsewhere later, and when they require more room.

Although potatoes succeed best with a little root-warmth all through the growing period, top heat, except what is afforded by the sun, is inimical to them, and should therefore be avoided by giving plenty of air on favourable opportunities, by tilting the lights at the back, so as to avoid cold currents, which, if allowed to pass through the frame while the leaves are young and tender, cause them to curl, and thus injure the crop. A month or so later on in the season, beds may be quickly made up by digging a shallow pit in the ground in which to put from 1 ft. to 2 ft. of fermenting material to give the potatoes a start, and carry them on till the weather gets warmer to finish them off. Places of this kind answer admirably to keep up a supply after those forced early are over, and by turning the manure and adding a little fresh about the middle of May, the frames may be most profitably utilized for growing summer melons, which, with early closing, ripen off well without much trouble or attention. Sunken beds such as these are well out of the wind, and therefore lie snug and warm, besides which, being low down, they are easily managed in the way of watering, covering up, &c., so that for late work they are all that can-be desired.

Even without such aid as a hot-bed affords, potatoes may be obtained a month or six weeks before they can be got from open borders, however warm and favoured their position may be. To do this, however, it is necessary to select a sheltered, sunny spot, where the soil is naturally light and dry, and then to make up a temporary frame by the use of any spare boards, to be either covered with straw, hurdles, or old lights, for the purpose of warding off frost and keen winds. Where turf can be had, a better and more permanent structure may be easily made, and one which will be found exceedingly serviceable for many purposes, as by the use of glass to lay on, any half-hardy plants may be safely wintered, or salads and a variety of other things grown in them. Next to brick, such frames are the handiest and most useful places any one can have, and the dead of the winter is a good time to build and turn them to immediate account, which can be most profitably done by starting with a batch of potatoes, and any light crop that may be required between.

The best kidney varieties for frame culture are the old Ashleaf and Myatt's, the former a fortnight or so the earlier of the two, but not nearly so productive or hardy, two qualities that render the latter much sought after, as they are of fine flavour, and excellent in other respects; indeed, for general purposes, they are about the most useful potatoes grown to afford a supply up to the middle of July, till which time there are none that surpass them, either for growing on the open borders, or under glass. Those who prefer round to kidney will find the Early Handsworth equal to any, and having short, close tops, they are suited for frame work, or growing close under the foot of a south wall. By planting these, or either of the foregoing, in a warm sheltered position of this kind, a good supply of new potatoes may be produced before the end of May, should the season turn out like anything favourable; and even if frosts occur, they can be easily protected by placing at night a few laurel or other evergreen branches in front. However grown, the great thing is to select good, sound seed, with strong, vigorous shoots, and these can only be obtained by laying the tubers out thin in some light, airy place, where they can come slowly on.

Potatoes for sets should never be more than one deep, for if they are, those below must inevitably have long drawn shoots, and these, under such circumstances, are sure to be bleached and tender, a condition in which they are easily susceptible of cold or wet, and this is one of the reasons why crops are so often defective. Anyone, therefore, having stores from which they intend to plant, should see to them in good time, because, when having begun to sprout, unless allowed plenty of room and kept cool, they soon take harm. For kidneys and all choice garden varieties, there is no better way of storing them than that of having shallow boxes, with bottoms formed of laths, nailed on 1 inch apart, between which the air has full play and strengthens the shoots as they form. Such boxes as these may be packed one on the other in any light shed, and a great quantity of potatoes may be thus stored in a small compass. In order to keep them apart, and admit air between, strips of wood should be nailed in the corner of each, or laid loosely across, so as to afford a distance of 2 inches or so, which, with the open bottoms, will be ample if the space in which they are set is kept as cool as possible.

It often occurs at the end of the season, after planting is over, that there are many more sets than are wanted, or that there are some left over from the general store, the largest and best of which may be turned to good account during the following winter. If these have the shoots rubbed out in the summer as they form, and are kept in a cool, damp cellar, they will, if buried in moist sand or soft soil, emit a quantity of young tubers around them, instead of forming any top growth ; and although these are not equal in point of flavour to such as are grown in frames, they are a great rarity at, or just after, Christmas. A boxful buried and put into any warm place about six weeks before they are wanted, will be found ready for use at any time, and as they do not require light, any one may have them indoors in a cupboard, or the corner of any spare room.

CHAPTER XII.

EXPERIMENTS WITH POTATOES.

There is often a danger of attaching undue importance to the results of experiments, and in devoting a chapter to the subject, we would preface it with this word of caution. So many, and sometimes such trivial causes apparently, operate to neutralize certain expected results; or, perhaps, some detail does not get that attention paid to it that it deserves, all of which help to detract from the real worth of any result that may be arrived at. Even where every detail has been diligently observed, perhaps on some occasions the result may be simply unaccountable. What may take place in one summer from following out a certain prescribed mode of treatment, may not result the next, although probably, to all appearance, every point may be as assiduously regarded as possible. An excessive rainfall, or a protracted drought, may exert an influence that causes the experience of one year to nullify that of another; or perhaps some slight difference—though not observed—in the manures employed on different occasions, brings about such varying results as to render it difficult to decide just how much reliance may be placed on any particular experiment, whether with potatoes or any other crop. Still we are by no means blind to the advantages that may arise therefrom, and those who on different occasions publish the results of any that have been carefully watched and accurately noted render a service to their brother workers in the same field. By any useful experience they gain at the cost of time, anxiety and expense, if they prevent others from following in dubious tracks, they do much good, and, if they succeed in setting at rest some long-disputed point by sheer diligence in the carrying out of any elaborately drawn schemes, deserve the thanks of others similarly engaged. We know what some of the leading features of successful potato-culture are; something about the soil that suits them best; what and when to plant, and how to treat the land before and after planting. From the fact, however, that very diverse plans are still adopted, and the potato-blight still commits its frightful ravages upon the crop, there is clearly much yet to be learnt upon the whole subject, by many who profess to grow this most commonly used vegetable. Whilst actual practice has satisfactorily proved what are some of the essential conditions to be observed in fairly successful culture, we may closely scan the many and varied results of experiments that are continually carried out, and appropriate such others of tried worth for our own benefit. Still the value of all such is obviously determined, not only by the perfect accuracy with which they are conducted, but by the frequency with which the same experiments are carried out. We give below a description of the manner in which a gentleman treated seed potatoes, together with the result; then a list of many varieties tested with a view of ascertaining their powers of propagation and their ability to withstand disease. In the next case we give an account of experiments with potatoes grown with various manures, and, lastly, we reproduce certain passages of the report of Mr. Davidson, last autumn, to the Chemico-Agricultural Society of Ulster, upon experiments made at Brookfield Agricultural School upon changing seed, manures, &c. First then, as regards the

Cutting Seed Potatoes.—The following is the pith of an address at Utica, by Director Sturtevant of the State Experiment Station, upon how to properly cut and plant seed potatoes. We quote from the *Country Gentleman*.

"The speaker began by calling attention to the following points:—

"1. A potato is covered with eyes which form the origin of the shoots. When the whole potato is planted in its natural condition, only two, three, or very rarely four, of these eyes vegetate. But rub and injure the eyes, or scald them slightly, and the number of the shoots is greatly increased; 15 to 30 will start from each eye, and often one eye will give as many sprouts as the whole potato would naturally have done. Nature seems to work at a great waste in potatoes, as she does in corn-pollen. 2. The common opinion is that, if the whole potato be planted, the strongest eyes will develop, the others remaining dormant. But who can tell which are the 'strongest' eyes? The fact is that if you plant a whole potato, and two or three shoots start, and you then rub off some of them, a great many more will appear, to take their place. 3. If you injure the eyes a little more deeply than is necessary to multiply the number of shoots, by pouring on boiling water, just avoiding killing the eye, then a mass of little *tubers* (15 to 25) will form instead of the shoot—illustrating the fact that a single eye has the capacity of originating all the potatoes that a whole plant ought to be expected to bear. 4. The new tuber is always borne above the seed. Sometimes the latter (all but the skin) is completely absorbed by the growing plant; sometimes you find it apparently almost unchanged.

"Now, the first absorption takes place *within definite lines* in the potato—which lines may be traced and studied by splitting the potato and soaking it in carmine water. It will be seen that a line of vital tissue, resembling cambium, runs through the centre of the tuber, with a branch running to each eye—which fact is of the highest importance. Tubers may form anywhere on one of these vital lines; the life of the potato is not confined to the eyes. This is strikingly shown by planting a whole potato with the eyes all destroyed, which will sometimes result in the formation of a new potato inside the old one, *without any vegetation whatever*, the old tuber shrinking as the new one grows. The practical lesson is : cut each eye deep to the centre, and at a certain definite angle to be ascertained by experiment, and you will get the maximum possible yield—best in quality also—from that eye.

"Trials of this plan in the field this year at the Station resulted as follows : A hundred hills were planted in rows a foot apart. Where whole potatoes, or halves, or quarters, were planted, there was no sort of uniformity in the yield ; the crop of adjoining hills varied as much as three to one. But where single eyes were planted, cut as above described, so as to preserve the axis of the eye, the product was surprisingly uniform in all the rows. In every case, the piece cut deep, however small, gave a much better yield and quality than a large piece cut shallow.

"In regard to the planting of potatoes, Dr. Sturtevant, early last spring started a number of eyes in sand in-doors, and grew them to 3 ft. in height, but they formed no tubers. When, however, they were transferred to the soil, they began immediately to form tubers. He judges that it is necessary that the temperature of the earth should be lower than that of the air in order that a crop may be produced. He has tried high hilling—4 to 5 ft. The result was few and very small tubers, because the plant had to do so much growing and digging. Yet deep planting is sometimes advantageous, for the tubers need a certain degree of protection, and sometimes in light soils the potato inclines to come a little toward the surface. Perhaps it seeks warmth and dryness. In one experiment, the addition of 6 in. of sand to an extremely heavy clay soil, utterly unfit for potato-growing, produced an extraordinarily large and fine yield.

"Essential conditions of success, then seem to be: 1. A single eye cut down to the central line; 2. Warmth and dryness for the growing tuber, but coolness and moisture for the roots. Proper cutting is the great point, everywhere and always. By this means the crop may be increased at least 25 per cent. over what it would be if the potatoes were cut in any other manner whatever; and there is great saving of seed besides."

The second experiment relates to the

Producing and Disease-resisting Powers of Potatoes.—Ireland last summer was prolific in potato experiments, in one instance as many as 80 varieties being tested to show their productive qualities and likewise their ability to resist disease. This experiment took place at the Munster Agricultural and Dairy School, and shows results as far as yield is concerned that few would probably expect. We give the list below of the varieties tested, with their yield, per statute acre, of marketable, small, and diseased tubers.

THE POTATO.

Variety.	Gross Yield per Statute Acre.				Marketable.				Small.				Diseased.			
	T.	C.	Q.	L.	T.	C.	Q.	L.	T.	C.	Q.	L.	T.	C.	Q.	L.
1. Early Pearl	16	1	1	0	14	10	0	0	1	1	1	0	0	10	0	0
2. White Star	7	12	2	0	5	18	0	0	1	13	0	0	0	1	2	0
3. Finure	8	1	0	0	5	18	0	0	1	15	0	0	0	8	0	0
4. Beauty of Hebron	6	6	0	0	5	8	0	0	0	12	0	0	0	6	0	0
5. Schoolmaster	6	8	2	0	5	6	0	0	1	0	0	0	0	2	2	0
6. Field Ashleaf	5	13	2	0	5	6	2	0	0	7	0	0	—			
7. Vicar of Lalcham	6	11	0	0	5	5	0	0	1	0	0	0	0	6	0	0
8. American Giant	5	18	0	0	5	5	0	0	0	6	0	0	0	7	2	0
9. Late Rose	6	8	2	0	5	3	0	0	1	5	0	0	0	0	2	0
10. Gloucestershire Kidney	6	2	1	0	4	17	0	0	1	2	3	0	0	2	2	0
11. American Magnum Bonum	6	9	0	0	4	17	0	0	0	19	0	0	0	13	0	0
12. Brinkworth's Victory	5	16	1	0	4	15	0	0	0	17	0	0	0	4	1	0
13. Block Apple	5	16	3	0	4	13	0	0	0	19	0	0	0	6	3	0
14. Brownell's Beauty	5	0	0	0	4	13	3	0	0	5	2	0	0	1	3	0
15. Reading Prolific	5	12	0	0	4	11	0	0	1	0	0	0	0	1	0	0
16. Regent	5	10	3	0	4	11	0	0	0	19	0	0	0	0	3	0
17. American Chili	5	9	3	0	4	10	3	0	0	19	0	0	—			
18. Red Skin Flourball	5	15	3	0	4	0	2	0	1	0	1	0	—			
19. Early Vermont	5	9	2	0	4	8	0	0	1	1	0	0	0	0	2	0
20. Purple Kidney	5	8	0	0	4	8	0	0	0	16	0	0	0	4	0	0
21. Pride of America	5	11	0	0	4	8	0	0	1	3	0	0	—			
22. Early Ashleaf	5	8	1	0	4	7	0	6	1	0	0	0	0	1	1	0
23. Queen of the Valley	5	0	0	0	4	6	2	0	0	3	2	0	0	10	0	0
24. Early Rose	5	16	0	0	4	6	3	0	1	8	0	0	0	1	1	0
25. Pride of Ontario	5	2	3	0	4	5	0	0	0	17	0	0	0	0	3	0
26. Red Fluke	5	2	0	0	4	5	0	0	0	17	0	0	—			
27. Pride of Ontario	5	0	3	0	4	4	0	0	0	16	2	0	0	0	1	0
28. Brinkworth's Beauty	5	5	2	0	4	3	1	0	0	19	2	0	0	2	3	0
29. Bressee's Peerless	5	3	0	0	4	3	0	0	0	14	0	0	0	5	0	0
30. Bluebard	5	1	0	0	4	3	0	0	0	17	0	0	0	1	0	0
31. Birbank	5	1	0	0	4	3	0	0	0	18	0	0	—			
32. Triumph	5	3	3	0	4	0	0	0	1	3	0	0	0	0	3	0
33. Prairie Seedling	5	0	0	0	4	0	0	0	0	13	0	0	0	7	0	0
34. Grosse Jaune	4	8	2	0	3	17	0	0	0	11	0	0	0	0	2	0
35. Reading Abbey	5	17	2	0	3	15	0	0	2	0	0	0	0	3	2	0
36. Waterloo Kidney	4	6	1	0	3	13	0	0	0	12	2	0	0	0	3	0
37. Reading Abbey	4	8	0	0	3	11	0	0	0	9	2	0	0	7	2	0
38. Late Fortyfold	4	17	0	0	3	11	0	0	1	6	0	0	—			
39. Fortyfold	4	8	2	0	3	11	0	0	0	16	0	0	0	1	2	0
40. Ash Top Fluke	5	0	2	0	3	10	0	0	1	10	0	0	0	0	2	0
41. Ruby	4	10	2	0	3	10	0	0	1	0	0	0	0	0	2	0
42. Early	4	9	0	0	3	10	0	0	0	12	0	0	0	7	0	0
43. Late Beauty of Hebron	4	19	2	0	3	8	2	0	1	0	0	0	0	11	0	0
44. Scotch Blue	4	0	0	0	3	7	0	0	0	11	2	0	0	1	2	0
45. Magnum Bonum	5	7	0	0	3	7	0	0	1	19	0	0	0	1	0	0
46. Striped Don	4	6	2	0	3	6	2	0	1	0	0	0	—			
47. American Triumph	4	0	2	0	3	6	2	0	1	0	0	0	0	3	0	0
48. Early Beauty of Hebron	4	9	2	0	3	6	0	0	1	2	2	0	0	1	0	0
49. Early White Rough Skin Rose	5	3	3	0	3	6	0	0	1	11	0	0	0	6	3	0
50. Early Snowflake	4	10	0	0	3	5	0	0	0	17	0	0	0	17	0	0
51. Alpha	4	5	2	0	3	5	0	0	0	19	0	0	0	1	2	0

Variety.	Gross Yield per Statute Acre. T. C. Q. L.	Marketable. T. C. Q. L.	Small. T. C. Q. L.	Diseased. T. C. Q. L.
52. Canadian Prolific	4 0 3 0	3 4 0 0	0 15 0 0	0 1 3 0
53. Porter's Excelsior	4 0 1 0	3 3 0 0	1 3 0 0	0 0 1 0
54. Fox's Seedling	4 15 0 0	3 3 0 0	1 13 0 0	—
55. Wonderful Ltd	3 4 2 0	3 2 0 0	0 2 2 0	—
56. Brown Black	4 18 0 0	3 0 2 0	1 16 0 0	0 1 2 0
57. Compton's Surprise	4 0 0 0	3 0 0 0	1 3 0 0	0 3 0 0
58. Brown Rock	5 6 1 0	2 10 2 0	2 0 0 0	0 0 3 0
59. Washington	3 19 0 0	2 19 0 0	1 0 0 0	—
60. Bresee's Bountiful	3 18 2 0	2 17 2 0	1 0 0 0	0 1 0 0
61. Pousse Debout	3 13 2 0	2 17 2 0	0 10 0 0	0 6 0 0
62. Grampian	3 11 2 0	2 17 0 0	0 14 2 0	—
63. Radstock Beauty	3 17 2 0	2 15 2 0	1 2 0 0	—
64. Oneida	4 6 0 0	2 14 0 0	1 12 0 0	—
65. Salmon Kidney	3 14 0 0	2 14 0 0	0 17 2 0	0 2 2 0
66. Davidson's Surprise	4 0 2 0	2 13 0 0	1 0 2 0	0 1 0 0
67. Lye's Favourite	4 0 0 0	2 13 0 0	0 11 0 0	0 16 0 0
68. Moray Blue	4 13 2 0	2 13 0 0	1 10 0 0	0 1 2 0
69. Quarantaine do la halle	3 16 3 0	2 12 2 0	0 19 3 0	0 4 2 0
70. Harrison's Early Rose	4 2 0 0	2 12 0 0	1 10 0 0	—
71. Wonderful Red Kidney	3 14 2 0	2 12 0 0	1 2 2 0	—
72. Beamishes	4 17 0 0	2 9 0 0	2 7 0 0	0 1 0 0
73. International	3 12 3 0	2 7 2 0	1 4 2 0	0 0 3 0
74. Snow Flake	2 4 1 0	2 3 1 0	0 0 3 0	0 0 1 0
75. River's Royal Ashleaf	2 17 2 0	2 1 0 0	0 15 0 0	0 1 2 0
76. Red Ashleaf	2 8 2 0	2 0 2 0	0 8 0 0	—
77. Garibaldi	2 2 1 0	2 0 0 0	0 1 1 0	0 1 0 0
78. King of Flukes	2 5 3 0	1 19 0 0	1 6 0 0	0 0 3 0
79. Peach Blow	2 19 3 0	1 17 0 0	1 0 0 0	0 2 3 0
80. Circassian	2 3 2 0	1 16 2 0	0 6 3 0	0 0 1 0

Now, by way of illustrating what we remarked above, it is important to know under just what conditions the seed of these many varieties was grown. If, for instance, some came off sand, loam, chalk, &c., but were all tested side by side upon any one description of soil—perhaps one of those named —the value of the experiment would be modified, inasmuch as this change of soil is all in favour of those potatoes that had the change and against others that did not. So likewise not only must the weight of the seed of each be carefully adjusted, but it is also important that each kind be subjected to the same treatment during the storing, and planted in equally as healthy a state as its competitor.

The third experiment illustrates the **value of sundry manures in potato-growing**, and was made on the Albert Model Farm, Glasnevin, near Dublin, under the supervision of Dr. C. A. Cameron, of Dublin. The trials took place on a portion of the experimental ground specially selected because of its state of exhaustion. The crop had thus to depend mainly upon the manures, so that their full effect could be more accurately ascertained than if the land were previously in good heart.

Four manures—namely, kainit, nitrate of sodium, sulphate of ammonia, and mineral superphosphate —were put to the test separately, as well as together in different forms. Nitrate of sodium applied at the rate of 2 cwt. per acre, costing £1 12s. and joined with 4 cwt. mineral superphosphate, costing 16s. produced a gross yield of 4 tons 5 cwt. per acre, of which 2 tons 11 cwt. were marketable, 1 ton 7 cwt. 2 qrs. small, and 6 cwt. 2 qrs. diseased, the percentage of dry matter in the sound tubers being 28·60.

Kainit by itself, 6 cwt. per acre, costing 14s. 6d., gave the highest gross yield—4 tons 13 cwt. 14 lb. per acre; 2 tons 6 cwt. 2 qrs. marketable, 2 tons 14 lb. small, and 6 cwt. 2 qrs. diseased, the percentage of dry matter in the sound potatoes 25·80.

Plot 3 is third with 1 ton 19 cwt. 2 qrs. per acre of marketable, 1 ton 12 cwt. small, and 2 cwt. 2 qrs. diseased potatoes, making a gross yield of 3 tons 14 cwt. per acre. The sound ones, showed 28:12

per cent. of dry matter. All the four manures were applied to this plot—2 cwt. (per acre, of course) kainit costing 5s. 6d., 1 cwt. nitrate of sodium, 16s., 1 cwt. sulphate of ammonia 2s., and 2 cwt. of mineral superphosphate 8s.—in all 6 cwt. of manure, costing £1 11s. 6d.

The plot dressed with 4 cwt. kainit, costing 11s., and 4 cwt. superphosphate, 16s., gave a higher gross yield, and only 2 cwt. less marketable tubers. It produced 4 tons 1 cwt. 2 qrs. per acre; 1 ton 19 cwt. marketable, 1 ton 14 cwt. small, and 8 cwt. 2 qrs. diseased, the dry matter in sound potatoes reaching 27·00. 8 cwt. per acre superphosphate alone, costing £1 12s., gave a gross yield of 3 tons 5 cwt. 2 qrs. per acre—1 ton 5 cwt. 2 qrs. marketable, 1 ton 19 cwt. small, and 1 cwt. diseased, with 27·04 dry matter in sound tubers. 2 cwt. sulphate of ammonia, costing £2 4s., and 4 cwt. superphosphate 16s., gave a gross yield of 3 tons 7 cwt. 2 qrs.—19 cwt. 2 qrs. marketable, 2 tons 2 cwt. 2 qrs. small, and 5 cwt. 2 qrs. diseased, with 26·10 per cent. of dry matter in sound tubers.

The other plots gave very poor yields—3 cwt. of sulphate of ammonia, costing £3 6s., only 8 cwt. 2 qrs. of marketable, and 1 ton 18 cwt. small potatoes; kainit, nitrate of sodium, and mineral superphosphate, costing £1 16s. 3d. per acre, 8 cwt. marketable, and 2 tons 11 cwt. small; kainit, sulphate of ammonia, and mineral phosphate, costing £2 2s. 3d. per acre, 8 cwt. marketable, 2 tons 3 cwt. small, and 1 qr. diseased; and 3 cwt. nitrate of sodium, costing £2 8s., only 6 cwt. 2 qrs. marketable, 2 tons 2 cwt.

2 qrs. small, and 1 cwt. diseased. An unmanured plot gave a yield of 2 tons 17 cwt. 2 qrs.; 1 ton 3 cwt. 2 qrs. marketable, 1 ton 9 cwt. 2 qrs. small, and 4 cwt. 2 qrs. diseased, with 26·90 dry matter in sound tubers. It will thus be observed that the manures used on the last four plots mentioned actually decreased the yield, instead of adding to it.

Some important conclusions may be drawn from these results. First, the great value of kainit (potash) as a manure for potatoes has received further striking confirmation. It will be seen that kainit alone gave by far the most profitable crop. It produced the heaviest gross yield—4 tons 13 cwt. 14 lb., at a cost of only 14s. 6d., the lowest outlay for manures on any of the plots. The potatoes therefrom were more watery and more of them small than those raised from a mixture of nitrate of sodium and mineral superphosphate, but while these two manures together produced 4½ cwt. more marketable tubers per acre than the kainit alone, they at the same time entailed a higher outlay to the extent of £1 13s. 6d. per acre. In other words the 2 tons 11 cwt. of marketable tubers from nitrate of sodium and superphosphate cost almost 1s. per cwt. for manure, while the 2 tons 6½ cwt. from kainit alone cost barely 4d. per cwt.—a gain of 13s. 4d. in favour of kainit. It will also be observed that the addition of kainit to superphosphate increased the total yield as well as the produce of marketable tubers, although the cost for the mixture of kainit and superphosphate was 5s. less than the cost of the dressing of superphosphate given alone. Nitrate of sodium and mineral superphosphate together answer pretty well for potatoes, but nitrogenous manures alone, and with certain others combined, do not answer at all. Sulphate of ammonia, costing £3 6s., produced 7 cwt. potatoes per acre, whilst nitrate of soda alone, costing £2 8s., yielded but 6½ cwt. marketable ones.

Regarding the proportion of diseased potatoes from the various manures, the experience of previous similar experiments does not tally exactly; in some cases the results are at variance with those of former years. Below we append a condensed Table which shows the chief results:—

Manure.	Cwt	£ s. d.	T. C. Q.	T. C. Q.	Total. T. C. Q.
Nitrate of sodium Mineral superphosphate	2½ 4	2 8 0	3 11 0	0 6 2	4 5 0
Kainit	6	0 14 6	2 6 2	0 6 2	4 13 0½
Kainit Nitrate of sodium Sulphate of ammonia Mineral superphosphate	2 1 1 2	1 11 6	1 10 2	0 2 2	3 14 0
Kainit Mineral superphosphate	4 4	1 7 0	1 19 0	6 8 2	4 1 2
Superphosphate	8	1 12 0	1 5 2	0 1 0	2 10 2½
Sulphate of ammonia Mineral superphosphate	2½ 4½	3 0 0	0 10 2	0 5 2	3 7 2
Sulphate of ammonia	3	3 6 0	0 8 2	...	2 6 2
Kainit Nitrate of sodium Mineral superphosphate	3 1 3	1 10 3	0 8 0	...	2 10 0
Kainit Sulphate of ammonia Mineral superphosphate	3 1 3	2 2 3	0 8 0	0 0 1	2 11 1
Nitrate of sodium	3	2 8 0	0 6 2	0 0 1	2 0 1
No Manure	...	...	1 3 2	0 4 2	2 17 2

The fourth set of experiments, with which we conclude this chapter, is, as before stated, described in a report of Mr. Davidson to the Chemico-Agricultural Society of Ulster, from which we extract the following:—

"In presenting to you the report of the experiments conducted on the potato crop under your direction at Brookfield Agricultural School, in order to prevent miscalculations by any portion of the public interested in such experiments, I may be permitted to state a fact of which you are well aware, but the general public is not—namely, that all possibilities of waste are excluded from these calculations; that an acre means every inch of land in an acre; and that no allowance is made for the necessary waste of culture, fences, or any other sources of deficiency; and that no part of the crop is considered beneath the care of calculation. A potato the eighth of an ounce in weight, although diseased, is carefully taken into consideration in the calculation of results.

Changing Seed—The advantage of changing seed is shown by the following: Skerry seed, grown on the same farm for several years, yielded per acre 6 tons 17 cwt. 3 qrs. 7 lb.; but new seed on the same ground yielded 7 tons 10 cwt. 3 qrs. 21 lb. per acre; and the increase of quality was exactly in the same proportion. The advantage of well-drained land over undrained has been very strikingly shown this year. Skerries, new seed, in undrained land yielded 7 tons 10 cwt. 3 qrs. 21 lb., but in drained soil yielded 8 tons 17 cwt. 21 lb. per acre. The

Champions, under similar conditions, in undrained land yielded 6 tons 11 cwt. 1 qr.; but in drained soil the yield was 8 tons 13 cwt. 3 qrs. 17 lb. per acre. The Magnum Bonum presents even a greater contrast. In undrained soil there was a yield of 4 tons 11 cwt. 3 qrs. 14 lb.; but in drained soil it was 8 tons 17 cwt. 21 lb. per acre. The difference in quality cannot be well shown in figures, but of picked potatoes suitable for market the undrained land yielded only 2 tons 12 cwt. 2 qrs.; but the drained soil yielded 6 tons 4 cwt. 2 qrs. 21 lb. It should be observed also that in undrained land the diseased tubers form a percentage of the refuse of all the lands; even of Magnum Bonum there were 6 cwt. 2 qrs. 7 lb. per acre of diseased potatoes.

Manures.—But of all the conditions which influence the production of crops over which the farmer has control, the action of manure appears the greatest. In a portion of the land where the crop was grown without manure, there was a yield of 3 tons 5 cwt. 14 lb. per acre; and in the same soil with the ordinary manure (about 25 tons per acre), the yield was 6 tons 17 cwt. 3 qrs. 7 lb.; but with extra manure, at the rate of 56 tons well rotted farmyard manure, the yield was 15 tons 8 cwt. 1 qr. 21 lb. per acre; but with the same heavy manuring on undrained soil, the yield was much less—8 tons 10 cwt. 2 qrs. 14 lb. per acre.

Varieties.—Of new kinds reared by Mr. Torbitt, and the seeds supplied for these experiments by Mr. A. Green, Truuira, a round blue potato like the Skerry, and named New Skerry, yielded 7 tons 17 cwt. 2 qrs. of good table potatoes, and 2 tons 19 cwt. 7 lb. of small ones, making a total of 10 tons 16 cwt. 2 qrs. 7 lb. per acre. This is a very superior potato in every respect, and free from disease. A white potato named **Tenant-right**, elongated, with a rather uneven surface, but good to eat, yielded 12 tons 9 cwt. 1 qr. 14 lb. per acre, of which 9 to 10 tons were suitable for table use; but in undrained ground the yield was only two-thirds of this. A very nice white potato, round shaped, remarkably free from disease or waste, and named **Gladstone**, yielded 7 tons 17 cwt. 2 qrs., and of these 6 tons 4 cwt. 2 qrs. were fit for table use; and an unnamed potato yielded 8 tons 10 cwt. 2 qrs. 14 lb. per acre, but being subject to disease would not be worth preserving.

To summarize these results, we find that the advantage of the potato crop of this year in drained land over undrained, all else being equal, is from 16 to 94 per cent., according to the kind of potato grown, and the difference between a light and heavy soil is almost in the same proportion. The advantage of changing seed is at least 11 per cent.; but the application of an increased quantity of manure gives a return so far beyond expectation that, without actual experiment it appears incredible."

CHAPTER XIII.

SPECIAL CULTURES.

1. London Market Garden Culture.—In the neighbourhood of London early potatoes are chiefly grown for market purposes, late kinds not being considered sufficiently remunerative to occupy such highly rented ground. The varieties usually cultivated are the old Ashleaf Kidney, Myatt's Ashleaf, Lapstone Kidney, and Regents. The ground selected for potatoes, if an open quarter, is usually the lightest and dryest at command, as in such soils the crop comes to maturity sooner than it otherwise would do, and tubers raised in such soils are of the best quality. About Deptford potatoes are planted in rows 2 ft. apart, the ground being previously manured and trenched, and levelled down with the harrow.

Planting takes place as soon after the middle of February as time and convenience will permit. Some growers plant two rows of potatoes between their lines of gooseberry and currant bushes, which are 6 ft. apart, and partially under the shade of large fruit-trees; but when fruit-bushes do not occupy this position, the potatoes are planted in continuous rows, about $2\frac{1}{2}$ ft. apart, just as they would be in open fields. Other market gardeners loosen the soil between the rows of their spring cabbages in March with a steel fork, and there plant potato sets with a dibber. When the potatoes appear above ground the cabbages are removed for market, therefore, little or no injury happens to either crop; and as soon as the potatoes get up a little and some earth is drawn to them with a hoe, the intervening space, if hard, is loosened with a fork, and again planted with Brussels sprouts or early sprouting broccoli. Before these can do much injury to the potatoes the latter will be ripe, when they may be lifted at once for market, or kept for seed or home consumption. In cases in which potatoes are grown in the open fields a crop of lettuces may be got from between them, but after these are removed, it is not considered well to plant anything else. No sooner are the tubers all lifted, than the haulm is collected and carted to the manure heap, and the ground is then manured, or not, according to circumstances, and ploughed or dug over, when it is ready for planting cabbage, coleworts, leeks, or for sowing with winter onions, spinach, radishes, turnips, or late celery. The summer culture of potatoes in market gardens consists in hoeing and keeping the crop rigidly clean. Potato crops are always earthed up—an operation which is done by means of broad iron hoes or double-moulded horse ploughs; and they are, as a rule, lifted with forks, but sometimes by the plough, which performs the task more expeditiously. The tubers, being collected and sized, are put into bushel and half-bushel baskets, and are covered with haulm, which is held in its place by means of twigs of hazel. These baskets are then piled one above the other in waggons for market.

With regard to general market potatoes, a correspondent writing to the *Gardener's Chronicle* in the early part of 1878 remarked:—

"When a grower of potatoes for market can undertake to rent for a short season of six months land for the purpose of growing potatoes for market at a charge of £13 per acre, it might well be asked, How are the profits to be obtained, and what kinds of crops are to be looked for? For this price the land is taken, well manured, and fairly well cultivated, the planter having the choice either of casting out drills with the plough or of dibbling the sets in. In the present case the former plan is adopted; the seed is laid in rapidly by women and boys, and ploughmoulders follow behind and cover in as fast as the sets are laid. A wooden roller presses down the apex of the ridges thus formed, and presently harrows will be run over the ground, and this will leave it in excellent condition for hoeing when the crop is well through the ground. The average quantity of seed per acre is about 30 bushels of small and 35 bushels of large. The present average price of seed of Victorias is 5s. per bushel, which, exclusive of labour, adds to the expenses about £8, and if £6 be added for labour and general cost per acre for lifting and other charges, it will make a total of £27 per acre, to be deducted from the value of the crop before there is any profit to go into the hands of the cultivator. Potatoes are a risky crop, late frosts may injure them, drought may check them, excessive moisture may provoke an undue amount of haulm growth and a severe attack of the inevitable disease. A good crop would be 8 tons per acre on ordinary fields, and from that may be deducted ½ a ton of chats worth about 15s. for pigs' food, and 1½ ton of seed size, leaving 6 tons of ware for market.

"This estimate will only be fulfilled if there be no disease, but if, as is too often the case, one-third be diseased, the largest tubers as a rule being the worst, then at most there will be but 4 tons of ware tubers for market, and only 1 ton of seed. The price of potatoes in the market is affected by the state of the crop, which, because of the immense extent of ground planted, is certain to be an abundant one if there be no disease, and the price then will range from £4 to £5 per ton. With a clean crop of Victorias held over until the market had settled down to its winter price at £5 per ton the amount realized per acre for 7½ tons would be £37 10s., and adding 15s. for the ½ ton of chats, £38 5s. A diseased year would give 5 tons at about £9 per ton, which would give a total of £45 15s.—a better paying crop, though less in bulk; but as the disease is so irregular in its effects it may be that this particular grower would not have more than one-half a crop clean for sale—a common result when the disease is very prevalent—and therefore it would not be safe to look in any case for a product that should realize more than £40 per acre under any circumstances. If from this be deducted the £27 per acre for expenses, and at least £3 for cartage to market, it will be found that £10 per acre is no great profit to look for out of such a venture, as all the amount deducted must be paid in hard cash before the crop can be marketed.

"In spite of all the contingent losses to which the cultivation of the potato for market is liable, it is evident that it is in market districts still one of the most widely grown and best paying crops. During the present winter, whilst turnips have been selling for a song and green stuff could hardly be given away, good potatoes have been fetching £10 per ton, and to have more of a vegetable that will certainly sell at a good price is the desire of all growers. Even so late as the end of March is comparatively early for the planting of potatoes in the open field, but Victorias are late growers, and therefore the safest to plant now. The more growers on a large scale recognize the desirability of planting the latest sorts first and earliest kinds last, the more probable is it that their crops will escape at least one of the potato ills—late spring frosts."

2. **Early Potatoes in Scotland.**—Potato culture in Scotland, whether of the early, medium, or late varieties, has long been regarded as one of the most profitable and at the same time one of the most speculative of crops the farmer can grow; but more especially is this applicable to the early descriptions, for it is only under exceptionally favourable conditions as to soil and season that a sound and heavy crop can be grown. There is no field crop that has

caused the rents of farms in Scotland situated in the more favoured districts to rise to such a high level as that of potatoes, and in almost every case the advance has been from 20s. to 40s. per acre, seeing that farms which previous to the Crimean War were rented at 30s. or 40s. per imperial acre are now 60s., 80s., 100s., and, in some instances, 140s. per acre. As a rule, early potatoes are grown in the West of Scotland, and more particularly in the counties of Ayr, Renfrew, Dumbarton, Bute, Wigtown, and Dumfries, their soil and climate being more favourable to their cultivation and early maturity than that of the eastern counties, which are almost entirely devoted to the production of the medium or later varieties. The latter are as superior in quality to those of the west as the early varieties of the west are to those of the east. The great struggle among all the large early potato-growers is to have potatoes in the market at the earliest possible time, and every imaginable method is adopted in manuring, planting, and variety to produce this result. For some years the districts around Girvan, in Ayrshire, and West Kilbride, in the same county, though somewhat further north, have been considered the very earliest in Scotland; next come those around the town of Ayr, the island of Bute, and parts of Wigtownshire; and, lastly, Dumbarton, Renfrew, and Dumfries, in the order named; for while the climate and soil of the latter county are possibly fully equal to Ayr, yet it has not the advantage of much seaboard, which the other counties possess in so large a degree.

Kinds.—We believe we are correct in stating that there are more than 400 varieties of potatoes, but there are not more than twenty that enjoy a favourable reputation, of which the early varieties in general cultivation are confined to four, these four being kidneys, Goodriches, Dalmahoys, and Red Bogs. Kidneys are not by any means largely grown, and the variety most in favour is that known as Myatt's Ashleaf. Goodriches are a sort that come very rapidly to maturity, all large growers planting a few acres to be ready for the very earliest markets; but the quality is very inferior, being soft and watery. The kinds most in favour, and most extensively cultivated, are the Dalmahoy and Red Bog, both, especially the latter, being heavy croppers, while the quality is all that can be desired. No potatoes are more appreciated in the great markets, and they are in much request by the English dealers. If the soil is in a proper state, and the climatic influences favourable, a commencement is usually made with planting in the very earliest districts about the beginning of February, and from this time every day is made the most of until the operation is completed, which, of course, entirely depends upon the weather, and freedom from frost and snow. The preparation of the land for receiving the sets is as follows:—The ground intended to be put under early potatoes receives a good deep ploughing of 8 or 10 inches in the autumn, and remains so turned over until the time previously mentioned (February 1), when a pair of heavy harrows are passed over it two or three times. If of a very light and friable nature, this harrowing is quite ample to reduce it to a sufficiently fine tilth; if dirty, and not so free and loose, a cultivator must be run through it once, possibly twice, and then it must be harrowed, the weeds collected, and carted off.

A double mould-board plough then commences to open up furrows to a depth of 6 or 8 inches, and a width varying from 24 to 30 inches, according to the peculiar ideas of the farmer, a general gauge being 7 inches deep and 27 inches wide. In these furrows or drills farmyard manure or, better still, seaweed (which, in the spring of the year is cast upon the beach in large quantities, and forms the very best manure that can be applied to early potatoes), is deposited, and spread by women with forks, a man following, and scattering guano, or other artificial fertilizers, over the dung or seaweed, and, lastly, women who place the potato sets over the manure, at regular intervals of about 9 inches apart along the drills. A second double mould-board or ridging plough then completes the operation by splitting the drills made by the first plough, and covering over the manure and potato sets. In this state they remain until the end of March or beginning of April, when, if the season is genial and early, the sets will be commencing to sprout and send out small buds or shoots, in which case it is necessary to harrow down the drills with what are called "saddle" harrows. These are very light, are drawn by one horse, and turn two drills at a time. In the course of another week the drills are again "run up" by a double-furrow plough, and harrowed down by the saddle-harrow a few days after. From the 10th to the 20th April the tender shoots ought to be appearing above ground, and a week afterwards hoeing should commence. This operation is performed by a small hand implement called a hoe, worked both by men and women, the object being to loosen the land all around the plants, and clean the drills. By the end of April the young potatoes should be seen in rows along the tops of the drills, on which the drill-grubbers or horse-hoes are run through, and the crop receives a first "earthing-up" by means of the double mould board-plough. In the course of a fortnight the drill-grubbers are again passed through, the double mould-board plough follows, a second heavy earthing-up is given, and the cultivation of the crop is completed.

Harvesting.—Having grown the crop, let us see when it is ready for harvesting or profit. If the season is an early and forward one, commencement with "digging" is made from the 10th to the 21st of June in the most favoured localities; if a late or backward one, nothing is done in this way until the beginning of July. Digging is performed with forks, or, as they are commonly called, grapes, handled by men, who throw the potatoes on to the top of the soil, the tubers being gathered and selected by women into three sizes—round, seconds, and small. The round and seconds are put into barrels and sent to market, and the small into bags for cattle and pig-feeding. Sometimes, if the potatoes are unusually early and digged in June, common turnips are afterwards sown, and a very fair crop raised; but if not as early, and digging does not take place until July, it is more advantageous to sow rape seeds among the potatoes a day or two previous to digging, the seed being covered as the potatoes are got out of the ground. This invariably produces a very heavy yield, affording excellent food for sheep in the autumn, and manurially enriching the land for a succeeding crop. Early potatoes are almost without exception sold to dealers at a certain stage in their growth, when both buyer and seller can form a reliable opinion as to their probable weight and quality. Six tons of early potatoes per imperial acre is considered a fair crop, eight tons a good crop, and ten tons a very heavy crop; indeed, it is very seldom that the latter weight is reached, and this only under very favourable circumstances. The price varies for the very earliest and best lots on the known farms from £32 to £36; for the secondary lots from £22 to £27; and for the third-rate, £15 to £22, all per imperial acre. Of course there are higher prices than £36 and lower than £15, but these are quite exceptional, and if a first-rate grower can net £25 to £27 per imperial acre on an average he is considered fortunate. When potatoes are sold per acre the dealer or purchaser pays all the labour except cartage to railway or steamer, which the farmer has to perform with his horses and carts. Another plan sometimes adopted is for the farmer to hire his land, horses, and men to the dealer, the latter paying him so much per acre, usually from £12 to £15, and supplying seed and artificial manure. One extensive Glasgow dealer grows annually from 400 to 500 acres under this arrangement. The Scotch early potatoes are sometimes disposed of in the Glasgow and Edinburgh markets, but by far the largest quantities are sent to the great English markets, where they are greatly esteemed, and command the highest current market rates.

3. **The Main or Late Crop of Potatoes in Scotland.**—The potato crop in Scotland is only inferior in importance to that of turnips, and in certain counties, notably East Lothian and Fife, is superior, but over the whole of the country turnips must take the first place. At the present moment we are not prepared with figures to prove the correctness of our statements, but there can be no question that both in point of extent and money value the turnip is the most important crop the Scotch farmer cultivates. We have already, in our description of the cultivation of the early crop of potatoes in Scotland, stated the fact that the early potatoes of the West of Scotland were as superior to those of the Eastern district, as the late potatoes of the East of Scotland were to those of the West, at which possibly some of our readers may express surprise; but the cause is not far to seek, and that cause is soil and climate. The soil of the East of Scotland from Berwick-on-Tweed

up to the north-east of Ross-shire is vastly superior to that of the western counties up to the same point west in Ross-shire, this large county running through from coast to coast, while the climate of the East, although colder, is much drier than the West.

Soils.—The soil best adapted for the growth of potatoes is a rich red loam, not too heavy, but of a medium texture. Such is met with around Dunbar, in East Lothian, where on a limited number of farms by far the finest potatoes, both in quality and colour, that can be grown in the kingdom are to be found. This district around Dunbar is certainly, in our opinion, the Garden of Scotland, and those who wish to see the finest farms that can be walked over should pay a visit to East Barns, two miles from Dunbar, consisting of 500 acres of the choicest land, and rented by Mr. James Hope from Mr. Mitchell, Innes, at £2,500 per annum, or £5 per imperial acre. The county of Haddington, as a whole, is particularly well adapted, both in soil and climate, for the growth of potatoes, and nowhere have rents risen to such a high level as here, which is entirely attributable to the prices which have been realized for potatoes in bygone years—many farms having, during the last twenty-five or thirty years, doubled their rents; but during the last two or three years a great change has taken place, seasons having been bad, and the potato crops have not only been inferior, but prices have been low; consequently a great many tenants have been ruined, and rents are falling rapidly. The counties of Forfar, Perth, Moray and Nairn, and Ross also, stand high as potato producers, and all of them have suffered severely from bad seasons and low prices, although not to the same extent as East Lothian.

Cultivation and Manuring.—Potatoes are almost invariably grown after a grain crop, although, as we shall afterwards describe, a feeling in favour of planting them after ley or grass is gradually extending, and, we think, with much benefit both to the land and to the crop itself. As soon as the harvesting of the grain crop is completed, all the manure that has been made about the farm buildings during summer is collected and spread upon the stubble at the rate of 20 or 30 tons per acre, the growers of this crop going in for very heavy management, and if within reasonable distance of a house or village the home supply of dung is supplemented by what can be purchased; for not only has the potato crop itself to depend upon the manuring, but the succeeding one of wheat, which usually follows, the former much exhausting the land. The whole of the fallow break—that is, land intended to be devoted to the growth of green crops in the following year—is then turned over as deep as possible with the plough, and so allowed to remain during the winter until the spring sowing of grain is completed, which is usually about the middle of March, when a commencement is made with preparing the land for potato-planting. If possible, this operation is completed by the middle of April. After the ground is reduced to a reasonably fine state—for potatoes do not require it to be as fine as most other root crops—the drills are formed by the double-mould plough from 28 in. to 33 in. wide, 30 in. being a very common gauge, and the portion which got no dung in the autumn now receives its full allowance, either direct from the heap which is usually collected in the field during frost in winter, or from the farmyard.

At the same time, a number of women who have experience are employed in cutting the potatoes into sets in one of the out-buildings; and it is very important that this is done carefully, otherwise a great amount of seed can be wasted, and the crop spoiled. Some potatoes will cut into three or four sets; but it is imperative that there are at least two eyes to every set, one not being sufficient to entirely rely upon. Some growers prefer to plant their sets whole, with only a small slice cut off the rose side, and for this "seconds" are used in preference to the large ones. Both methods have their advocates, but it is not a bad practice to use the seconds, provided they have two good eyes, as they have been tested side by side with large ones cut into sets, and the results have fully justified a continuance of the practice. While on the question of seed, we may here remark upon the importance of a frequent change of potato seeds, as few good growers use the same more than twice, while many change every year, believing that the increase in the weight and soundness of the succeeding crop much more than compensates for any extra expense that may be incurred. We quite agree with them. Every change of seed is not advisable—for instance, from a red dry soil to a cold clay or heavy loam; but *vice-versâ* will answer very well, while the best change of all is from virgin soil or moss to what may be termed rich potato land; in other words, a change from a poor to a rich soil will succeed; but the reverse will not hold good.

After the manure is spread in the drills, according to the quantity the farmer may deem desirable and the condition of his field, a certain amount of guano or prepared potato manure, say 4 cwt. to 8 cwt. per acre, is scattered above the dung in the drills. The potato sets are deposited, and the plough, splitting the original drills, covers in manure and seed. As previously mentioned, the practice is increasing of planting potatoes after ley, or after the field has lain in grass or pasture for three or more years, and this is done by what is called "trenching" the land, in the following manner; at the same time it must be remembered that this method is only applicable to real potato land, for it will not succeed on strong and retentive soils:—The field having been pastured by stock during the summer, it is laid off into breaks, and plough No. 1 makes an opening and one clear furrow, when plough No. 2 is introduced with a wheel attached, preventing it taking a greater depth than 3 in. or 4 in. off the surface, which skimming is thrown into the bottom of the furrow made by plough No. 1, which now follows plough No. 2, taking a furrow of at least 8 in., and through the soil into the top of the skimming cut by it. Plough now follows plough until the field is completed. The land remains in this loose state until the time for planting arrives, when two or three harrowings are all that is necessary to make it ready for drilling.

The advantages of this system are—1st, a great saving of time at a very busy season of the year ; 2nd, beyond about 10 cwt. per acre of guano and bones no heavy or farmyard manure is required—the surface sod which was turned down in the autumn, with the droppings of horses, cattle, and sheep for years, having rotted by the time planting commences, forms as good a manuring as at least twenty cartloads of dung to the acre (of course, after the potatoes are taken up, a good dressing of dung is given to put the land into proper condition for the succeeding crop, which is almost invariably wheat; but this is preferred to giving the dung for the potatoes); 3rd, after this trenching process the land is very easily managed for the rest of the rotation, being rendered free and loose, while there is no trouble from couch or other noxious weeds ; 4th, and last, the potatoes are much drier, of better quality, and much less liable to disease than those grown upon wet and raw manure—at any rate, the dealers will always give more for them, either per ton or per acre, than those grown in the ordinary way. About a fortnight before the potato shoots appear above ground the drills should be harrowed down, so as to let the plant get through more quickly, and obtain the benefit of the sun and air. As soon as they are fairly through the ground, the drill grubbers are run through, and the plants are then hoed and cleaned. Shortly afterwards the grubbers are again run through; the double-mould plough follows, and a shoulder is run up to the side of each drill, in which state they remain for another fortnight or three weeks, when a final grubbing and earthing up is given early in July; and so the crop remains until lifting time.

Harvesting.—Potatoes ought to be ripe about the beginning of October, when a beginning is made with lifting, which is sometimes done with the plough, sometimes with the fork, as in the case of early potatoes, and on all large holdings with the potato-raiser, drawn by two horses, which goes underneath the potatoes and by a side motion throws the potatoes on to the surface of the land. The potatoes are then gathered by men and women, put into carts which are placed in convenient positions in the field, and taken to the place where it is intended to pit them, to be sorted by women. The best are put into one pit, the seconds into another, while any small or diseased are taken to the homestead at once, to be consumed by the stock. The pits are usually about 4ft. wide at the base, and the potatoes are thrown up in an angular form to a sharp top, until no more will lay either on the sides or top, the sides being as sharp and slanted as possible, on which a layer of dry well-drawn wheat straw is placed about 8 in. thick, above which a covering of a similar thickness of soil is spaded on, leaving the tops of the pits uncovered except by straw for a week or ten days to allow any heat to escape, after which the tops are closed up, and tiles inserted on the sides of the pits, with mouths down, at intervals of about 2 yards apart. In this way the potatoes remain all winter; but if very severe frost should set in, the mouths of the tiles must be stopped and rough manure from the cattle courts spread over the pits. The potatoes are sent to market as prices and other considerations warrant, and the last are usually taken from the pits before the middle of April, when it is necessary any remaining should be removed from the pits and placed in an open and cool house, to prevent sprouting as much as possible. It is necessary that the potatoes should be pitted in a thoroughly dry state, otherwise they will rot and mould in; and further, they must be turned over in the pits at least twice during the winter.

Varieties.—There are a great many varieties of potatoes, but those almost exclusively planted in Scotland for the main crop are Dalmahoys, Red Bogs, White Regents, Red Regents, Paterson's Victorias,

Champions, and Skerry Blues. Until within the last three or four years the Regent was by far the most extensively cultivated and appreciated, but with the ominous seasons of 1872, 1877, and 1879, a great change has taken place in favour of Champions and Victorias, which are hardier and not so liable to disease, although we very much doubt if, on good soil and in a fine season, any potato can come up to the Regent in flavour and quality, besides which, on fine soils and well manured, it is a great cropper. Dalmahoys and Red Bogs are both very much appreciated, but they require the best class of potato soils to produce them to perfection, and the former is not a very heavy cropper yet subject to disease; while the latter is a much more robust and hardy variety, besides being a free cropper. Victorias are very extensively grown, and the Dunbar Victorias are considered the finest potatoes grown, but the objection to them is that they are a very expensive kind to grow, so far as seed is concerned, there being few eyes in them, and it takes one-third more to plant an acre than the other sorts. Further, they are very shy in coming through the ground, being frequently blanky; and, lastly, they are not prolific. The Champion is the latest variety, and is now very extensively grown, the peculiarity about it being that in a wet and cold season, when all other sorts are a failure, it succeeds best—indeed, its quality and flavour are better in a wet than in a dry season. Though coarse in appearance and deep in the eyes, it is nevertheless a good table potato, as also a great

L

cropper and most robust grower on all soils, fifteen tons per acre being no uncommon yield in favourable seasons, while another advantage is, that it requires a minimum allowance of manure to produce a full crop. It is supposed to be a cross between a Victoria and a Regent, but at any rate it is a great acquisition to potato-growers, for in the years 1877 and 1879 it saved many a struggling farmer from ruin. Skerry Blues are a coarse variety, but good croppers, and are only grown on the poorest class of soils and on small holdings.

Prices and General Remarks.—There can be no question that the potato is the most speculative crop grown by farmers, being uncertain alike as to yield and value, so much depending on seasons and prices. Some years dealers pay as much as £50 per acre for them, and £10 per ton, while in others not more than £10 or £12 per acre can be obtained, and 30s. per ton. Take, for instance, the season of 1882, when we are correct in stating that hundreds of acres of crop 1881 were sold at not more than £12 per acre, and 25s. and 30s. per ton. The reason of this was that the potato crop of that year was the largest and soundest that had been grown for the previous twenty-five years, consequently the supply was larger than the demand, and hence we saw for the first time the strange anomaly of thousands of tons of potatoes being shipped to New York, the price there affording dealers a nett profit of 15s. per ton after paying all expenses. Prices having, however, fallen on the other side, as the season became advanced farmers could be seen using

PRICES AND GENERAL REMARKS. 147

up large quantities for cattle and pig-feeding, in order to get them consumed. Speaking of prices of potatoes, there was a field on the farm of Skateraw, near Dunbar, and closely adjoining the farm of East Barns, previously mentioned, containing as many as fifty acres, for which a dealer paid Mr. Nelson, the tenant, the handsome sum of £2,500, or £50 per acre. After purchasing this field the same dealer shortly afterwards came to East Barns, examined the potato crop, and offered £40 per acre, at which Mr. Murray was highly indignant, saying that he would not take £49 19s. 11¾d.! This story came from Mr. Murray himself, so was without doubt accurate. In a good year as many as 10 or 12 tons per acre of marketable potatoes will be lifted on well managed farms, while in the following year, not as favourable, not more than 4 or 5 tons.

Again, prices vary from £2 to £10 per ton. Sometimes a sudden turn in a market means a loss or gain of several hundreds of pounds to farmer or dealer; one notable instance being in the spring of 1880, for it will be remembered that the season of 1879 was a very wet one, and the Irish potato crop was a failure, while the finer qualities in Scotland were completely destroyed by disease. From October, 1879, until February, 1880, the prices of potatoes remained stationary at from £5 to £6 per ton, but about the beginning of February, 1880, a great demand for seed of the Champion variety set in for Ireland, thousands of tons being shipped from Greenock to Dublin and other Irish ports, and in one fortnight prices rose from £5 and £6 per ton to £10 and £12, or just double, so that some farmers who were fortunate enough to hold on, and dealers holding large quantities, realized handsome sums. In 1879 the yield of Scotland was not more than one-half of what it was in 1880 or 1881, and yet the price was so much higher that the crop was of considerably greater value, some farmers obtaining for the crop of 1879 £50 per acre, while one large farmer could show a field which the one year it was under potatoes realized £60 altogether and the other over £1,000. There can be no doubt that since 1872 potato-growers have had a bad time of it, and it is very doubtful if, during the interval, they have paid. One, speaking from experience of the subject, says they have not, that when the high rents, heavy labour and manure bills, and the price of seed (the latter often costing £5 per acre) are taken into account, it is difficult to see where the profit is, more especially when a risk of disease is considered. Altogether potatoes cannot be grown on the best class of farms under £20 per acre, so that anything received over and above this sum on an average of years may be regarded as profit.

In conclusion, as showing the importance of the potato crop in Scotland, we believe there are something like 280,000 acres grown annually, the largest producing three counties being Perth, with about 21,500 acres; Fife, with 18,600; and Forfar, with 18,300, so that these three counties alone produce annually about 58,400 acres, representing a money value approaching a million and one quarter sterling.

4. How Early Potatoes are grown in Lancashire.—The following is from the pen of the late Mr. Williams, of Ormskirk :—" I live in a part of the country where nearly a whole parish, and portions of several others, are occupied in growing early potatoes in a manner scarcely known, I think, elsewhere, and certainly worthy of imitation where this vegetable is largely required. Cottagers, large and small farmers, and nearly every occupier of land, have more or less to do with their production; and when I tell you that £70 was offered for the early potatoes growing in a cottage-garden, on a piece of land that would not half support a cow, and that some of the growers have about a quarter of a mile, or upwards, of pits for the purpose (they are grown in pits), the affair must be considered important; so much so, that I have often wondered that the custom is so local. Perhaps when I mention that the neighbourhood where these early potatoes are grown adjoins the district where the potato was first cultivated in England, the subject may be rendered more interesting. The early potatoes are grown in turf pits, covered with straw screens that are made in a peculiar manner. To the making of these screens I shall first direct attention, and in order to render my description more intelligible, I have prepared a few sketches of the process. First, then, make a strong frame, 6 ft. by 4 ft., which shall, when shut, resemble a monster kind of book-cover in two parts, which are hinged together strongly at the back and fastened with hooks and staples where the book-clasps would be (fig. 1). The pieces forming the back, where the hinges are

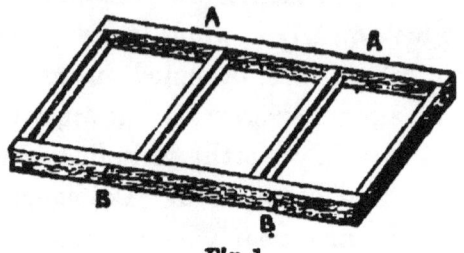

Fig. 1.

placed, and the front, where the bolts are used, should be of oak, 2½ in. thick, and 6 in. wide. A piece at each end, and two in the middle, also of oak or ash, 1 in. thick, are let into the pieces forming

Fig. 2.

back and front, leaving between the "boards" a space 3 in. deep, which is intended to contain the material of the screen, or what would be the letterpress of a volume. Procure two tressels on which to place the frame—each tressel, when in position, having a post, or stout piece of wood, 6 ft. high, let firmly into the ground at its end as (fig. 3). When the frame is laid on the tressels, one part is turned up and fastened to the posts as at (fig. 2). On the part of the screen that lies on the tressels, prepared pieces of tough branches of wood, such as hazel, oak, dead spruce, larch, or any durable young wood, are laid, and on the toughness of the brush employed depends the durability of the screen.

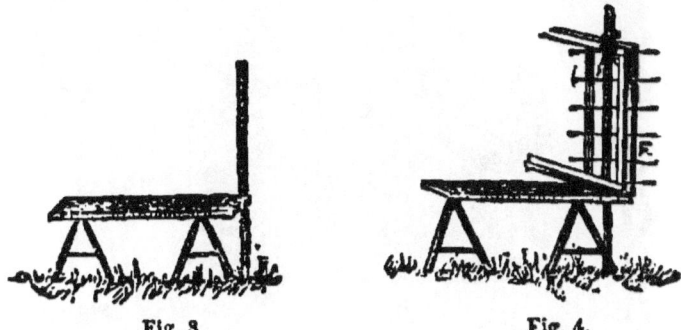

Fig. 3.　　　　　　　Fig. 4.

Such spray as that of beech, elder, &c., is of no use, as it only lasts one season, and when the wood is worn out the screen is comparatively useless. Now place on the wood long wheat straw, to the thickness of about 1 in., equalizing it over the whole frame, and making both ends full. More branches of a stronger kind are then laid on, keeping some of the straighter pieces for the outsides, and using three strong pieces cross-ways to give strength. It is this middle enclosed brushwood that gives a firmness to the whole, and makes the screen as solid as a table-top. Add another layer of straw as before, on which place some of the flatter and lighter pieces of spray, as at first. Now bring down the turned-up part of the frame, and bolt together as at (fig. 1.) Some amount of pressure will be required, owing to the mass of straw and wood employed, but this gives firmness to the screen. Turn the whole of the screen up to the two posts (fig. 4), to which it is fastened at the top, the lower part still resting on the tressels. Tarred twine must now be in readiness, with two needles made of hard oak, 1 ft. long

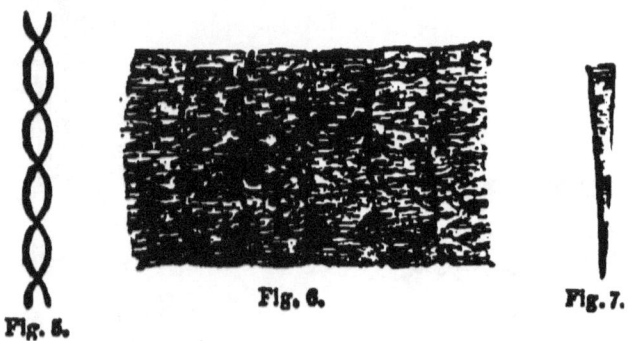

Fig. 5.   Fig. 6.   Fig. 7.

(fig. 7), with perforated eyes, and a man on either side of the screen passes them through in three or five places, as at E (fig. 4), exchanging needles at every stitch, thus forming a kind of brace-stitch (fig. 5). When this operation has been completed, twist off the ends of the brush and straw flush with the ends of the frame, and you have the screen represented in (fig. 6.) Although I have merely alluded to these appliances as being largely used for early potato growing, they are amongst the most useful articles in a garden. Placed at an angle of

45° over celery rows, they would effectually protect them from wet and snow. Round early-made hotbeds they are also invaluable. Supported on bricks over parsley beds they afford protection in all weathers, and neither staking nor nailing down will be required. Early vine borders may be thatched over with them, and three or more placed around shrubs will afford them a neat and efficient protection. Many other uses will suggest themselves. Temporary pits to any extent may be made with them; or, by laying them end to end, tied to stakes, they furnish capital places for hardening-off bedding plants. They can be made by any labourer, and stowed away, when dry, under a shed, will last for years. Where used extensively by the potato growers they are made into stacks and slightly thatched over till wanted.

"I will now proceed to explain the method of raising the potatoes. These are grown in pits made of turf. The best and most sheltered situations adjacent to the dwellings of the growers are chosen; a good thick hedge running east and west is a good site, or a sheltered piece of land is often wholly occupied by a series of pits running parallel to each other; in short, naturally warm places are always chosen, and if they do not exist they are artificially made so. The pits are constructed of any required length from the sods on the place. The walls are 1 ft. thick, 1 ft. high at the back and front, and 4 ft. high at the ends or gable; they are about 8 ft. wide; a slight rail, answering to the ridge tile of a building runs the whole length, supported, where necessary, by upright pieces, which, of course, run down the centre of the pit (fig. 8 A). A more slender rail, or even tar twine fastened to upright sticks, runs parallel with the ridge piece, midway between it and the walls, both at the back and front (as at B). Of course a slight rail is preferable to the twine, where obtainable. The use of the latter is to prevent the screen (one end, of course, resting on the wall and the other on the ridge piece) from swagging downwards with the weight of wet or snow.

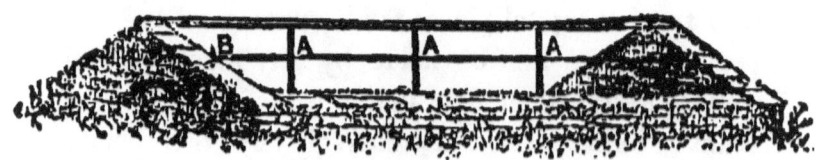

Fig. 8.

" I will now suppose the pit to contain a sufficient quantity of highly manured soil, and to be ready for planting. The most important matter, however, in the whole affair is the preparation of the sets, and this is peculiar and totally at variance with the directions usually given for the sprouting process of growing early potatoes. The system generally advocated is to push the set into growth only for 2 in. or 3 in. and then by exposure to green the sprout. In the method I am now endeavouring to describe, the main point is to keep them white and tender, just as they would be when buried in the soil; and the theory is, that this is effected by keeping the sprout continually growing from the first. Any greening or hardening is considered detrimental, and a waste of time. On consideration, it will be evident that a potato sprout that is greened and hardened before planting must become blanched and softened before it commences to grow. Laying down—that is, putting the potatoes to sprout—commences about Christmas Day. A hay-loft or barn floor, or any spare room, is used for this purpose. Selected medium-sized whole potatoes are used, and placed as close together as they can be packed singly. Bricks or pieces of wood are placed at convenient distances as the potatoes are laid down, serving as alleys. On these slight strips of wood are placed over the sets, and the whole is covered over with stout paper, such as old

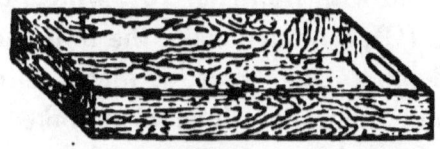

Fig. 9.

newspapers, &c. This is done to exclude light and air, and acts as a kind of forcing process with the potato. Hay or litter is placed over the paper in frosty weather. This method is a rather dangerous one in hard frost, especially so in a very severe winter. A modification of it, certainly to be preferred for general purposes, is to use light-made 9 in. deep boxes, 4 ft. long and 2 ft. wide, with no tops (fig. 9). These are filled with potatoes, as on the floors, and are piled one on the other in any convenient place. Being all of one size, the bottom of one serves as a top to the other. Old orange-boxes are well adapted for this purpose, and do well where they can be had. The sets, by this method, can easily be protected from frost, as, in extreme weather, they can be carried anywhere—they are sometimes put in rooms under beds.

"Planting time commences on Valentine's Day, the screens having been placed on the beds a few days previously to keep the soil dry, and the sets are uncovered on the floors or in the boxes for about three days, to give the sprouts a certain firmness. They are cut up as planted, each set having one good sprout about 6 in. long. Scrupulous care is taken to reject every sprout with a hard or black point. Holes are made all over the bed, 9 in. every way, with a kind of dibble shod with iron (fig. 10), which, owing to a cross-piece (C), can only make the hole the required depth. One potato is placed in each hole, and then the whole pit is raked carefully over with a wooden rake or hay-rake, which, as the sprouts are barely $\frac{1}{2}$ in. below the surface does not break the points. The back screens are then put on from end to end, the ends on the ridge being kept true to each other, so that the front screens, when put on, form a good lap on the back ones. The work, as far as planting goes, is now done, and, as the potatoes have had no check, they are up directly. The front screens are taken off every warm, sunny day that comes, and put on early in the afternoon, always according to weather—and now the care begins. No sunny day must be lost, and a frosty hour would be fatal. It would be useless for any one

Fig. 10.

to attempt growing potatoes largely on this plan
except he can afford to have some person nearly
with them. Small farmers or cottagers, with always
stout lads and lasses, generally follow it. A ton of
screens to lift off in the morning, and put on again
in the evening, is labour, and those who cannot
afford cheap labour do not attempt it. The back
screens are seldom taken of till the potatoes are far
advanced, or when rain would be beneficial, and the
front ones, when taken off, are laid down sideways,
tile fashion, but always below the level of the front
wall, so that a single ray shall not be intercepted.
The back screens being kept on, not only keep the
cold and the winds away, but prevent the heat
entering on the enclosed or open side from being
lost by radiation. It is a strange sight to see these
potato beds up and green in the open air in April.
The potatoes are ready early in May, and are packed
in neat hampers, each containing 20 lb., which
sometimes realize 1s. per lb., and which is thought
a good price. They are bought up by dealers, who
convey them to the manufacturing towns, Bolton,
Barnsley, Blackburn, or Manchester, and quite an
ovation is paid to the person who takes the first
consignment to market. Inn-keepers, shop-keepers,
and others present him with pieces of ribbon of
every possible pattern and colour, which are pinned
on every available portion of the dress, so that I
have seen these men come back from the market
thatched, as it were, with ribbons.

"Thus I have described at length, but I trust

clearly, the practice followed to a very great extent by cottagers and small farmers. Gardeners will at once see the value of this system as the means of raising an intermediate crop between those grown under glass and warm borders in the open ground, and there is no doubt that these pits in large gardens could be utilized for other crops after the potatoes. What a charming place for salading in parching summers, and what capital places to protect such plants as lettuce, or cauliflower, till the middle of February! No such use, however, is made of them by the potato growers. When the potatoes are off, the soil is thrown up into a high side, from end to end, and remains so till planting time comes round again."

5. **Potato Growing in Jersey.**—The culture of the potato in this island is one of, if not the leading feature of agriculture, and for the early produce a ready and remunerative sale is found at our London markets. The following interesting sketch was lately published in *Land*:—

"How many of the English and French excursionists who, in the height of the tourist season, do their best to turn Jersey into a peripatetic music-hall, are aware that the charming little island is a large exporter of potatoes? The rent is paid by potatoes elsewhere than in Ireland, as the jolly Jersey farmer will tell you if you ask him, with a pitying shrug for your ignorance. The month of June, a few weeks before the excursion season eaches summer height, is the time when the hard-working Jersey cultivator is busier than ever with his potato crop.

"The extent to which tubers are cultivated in the island is strikingly shown by the following comparative table. The estimate is in *vergées*, a Channel Island land measure, of which two and a quarter go to the acre :—

Parish.	Vergées under wheat.	Under potatoes.	Under orchard.
St. Heliers	338	800	202
St. Saviour	500	990	200
St. Martin	483	935	350
Trinity	608	1,177	509
Grouville	324	603	323
St. Clement	210	537	127
St. Lawrence	628	1,130	353
St. Peter	474	1,078	161
St. Brelade	316	605	47
St. John	628	948	386
St. Mary	332	634	149
St. Ouen	608	1,770	134

"It will thus be seen that the parish of St. Ouen (or St. Owen) is the largest, though not the most populous, and far from the most productive, except at one sheltered spot on the coast called Etac, where the potato crop is fine and early.

"These three, potatoes, wheat, and fruit, are the leading items in Jersey agricultural produce. During the spring and early summer there is but one topic of thought through the island—viz., the potato crop —and even the casual visitor becomes infected with the symptoms, and finds himself taking great interest in the number of tons that pass each day over the weighbridge. In sober earnest, however, the potato trade in Jersey has assumed an enormous magnitude, for it is only of late years that potatoes have been exported from the island in anything like their present bulk. The last decade has shown the capabilities for cultivation so conclusively, that everything else is now subordinate to it. Fruit, which was once a great Jersey staple, has declined, and even Jersey apples, once grown in quantities for cider-making, are now almost things of the past, the fact being that the orchards in all directions are cut down to make room for potato ground, which is somewhat of a suicidal policy. In consequence of the rapid utilization of the soil, land has greatly gone up in price, the average being about £12 an acre. In some parts of the island, as Etac, two crops of potatoes are obtained every year, although this is by no means universally the case. The manure used is the *craic*, or seaweed, the harvesting of which is an occasion of considerable importance, so much so that the operations are regulated by law. At any time of the year, however, the coast farmer may gather what is called the *vraic de venue*, or chance seaweed that may be floating about the rocks, which is hauled in by long rakes. *Vraic* makes excellent manure, and the burnt ashes are good top dressing.

"The fluctuations of the potato trade are remarkable, and a grower who has sent his cart full of potatoes to the wharf at St. Heliers is quite uncertain what he is to get for them, except, perhaps, when he is his own consignee, and deals direct with the London purveyor. But in the great majority of cases the trade remains in the hands of the potato merchants, who are either resident in St. Heliers or have establishments there, as well as at Goole, Hull, Leeds, London, Liverpool, and the principal centres of population. The potatoes are invariably sold by the *cabot*, a Jersey weight equivalent to 40 lbs. English, or 37 lbs. Jersey, there being 52 cabots and about 14 ounces over, to a ton. The early growers will get high prices, from 7*s.* to 8*s.*, 9*s.*, or 10*s.* per cabot, the very first produce of the season realizing fancy prices for small parcels of a few pounds each. But when the season is advanced from 2*s.* 6*d.* to 3*s.* per cabot is the average, the fluctuations occurring from glut in the market, over-speculation, or absence of steamers. The farmers who send their supplies in the morning may get 4*s.*, or even more, while by the afternoon prices may have dropped a shilling.

"The potatoes are dug principally by Bretons, who, men, women, and boys, flock over at this time of the year, and supply the needful labour at about 1*s.* 6*d.* per diem. From every parish and hamlet come the potato carts—long vehicles, something like a piano van cut away lengthways—and each full of casks, crates, or anything available for bringing the potatoes from the ground to the wharf. As the lanes debouch into the high road, the procession of carts becomes interminable, and by the time that St. Heliers is reached, a string of nearly a mile in length will be waiting their turn at the weighbridge. The gross weight is first taken, after which the driver takes his load and empties it into a merchant's store, returning again to the weighbridge to have his cart weighed, after which he receives his money. By night it is far more dangerous to cross the open to the pier, than it is to cross Oxford Circus, for although every driver is compelled by law to have a side light, on penalty of half-a-crown, a good many evade it and drive off home in a rather reckless manner. In the last week of June no less than twelve steamers were generally loaded in one night, and 3,000 tons of potatoes are not an uncommon amount to pass over the weighbridge in a day. To show the increasing character of the trade, it is sufficient to mention that while the export in 1880 was 33,043 tons, that of 1881 was 38,596, while the results of the past year were considerably over 40,000 tons. The decline of the fruit trade is shown by the fact that the exports were 36,056 and 30,291 tons respectively for 1880 and 1881."

CHAPTER XIV.

GROWING POTATOES FOR EXHIBITION.

WITH the growing popularity for most kinds of shows, both agricultural and horticultural, a treatise upon potatoes could scarcely be considered complete unless a chapter were devoted to the proper way of growing them for exhibition. Any one who has seen the hundreds of dishes decorated with tubers of all kinds, sizes, shapes, and colours at the International Potato Show at the Crystal Palace, must have noticed what care had evidently been bestowed upon their growth, selection and preparation, &c. From Mr. Porter's interesting pamphlet upon "How to Grow Potatoes with Success for Exhibition" we have taken the following extracts, and would recommend those whose object is to grow mainly for show purposes to read his little book themselves, since what he advances on this particular phase of potato culture is the result of very successful experience therein.

"THE SOIL.—It is very important that the soil should be friable and well pulverized, and to secure this it must be thoroughly wrought; and the sub-soil should also be well broken to prevent so far, in this way, the crop from suffering by over-drought or stagnant moisture. But though it is important to have good, well-pulverized and suitable soil, still, if my instructions as to seed and planting are attended to, considerable success may be attained by growing in any soil almost—even in what has been termed the 'riddlings of creation.' One thing, however, is especially to be avoided—and that is, old lime rubbish. Yet, while speaking thus, I do not mean that it is unimportant to have good soil. Stiff clay is not suitable, and where this exists, let good friable mould be supplied by all means to intermix, and in particular to surround where the tubers form. It is of the utmost importance to get clear of stones and hard and knotty substances, so far as not to come in contact with the forming tubers, else perfect shapes cannot be expected. It is not necessary, however, to clear away stones generally, if only they are kept from contact with the tuber-beds, for they not only draw heat, but also tend to conserve moisture. It is of great importance to grow after old lea, if this can be had, but in this case the first year is not the best, as the full advantage can be obtained only when the turf is well-broken and decomposed. If the land has been a number of years in lea before breaking up several successive crops may be grown with much success.

"Seed.—The selecting and preparing the tubers intended for seed is a very important matter. In the first place see to have the best competition varieties; and, when desiring a change of seed, get, if possible, from a colder climate; but with reference to American sorts (so-called), it is good for a change to obtain seed direct from America..... I have proved that to get tubers direct from America is highly beneficial, but from my own experience generally, I have considered it unadvisable and unnecessary, as a rule, to obtain a change of seed, unless by growing my own selected potatoes myself in different soils; and for one reason, that had I changed seed otherwise I should have lost the advantages gained by continued selection, and improvements thus secured, and by my own methods of cultivating.

"Select the seed from well-grown crops, and if so done, there is no need for using the largest tubers. Take moderate-sized, and even under-sized ones, if to plant whole, which I have found best. Lay out all the tubers for prize growing on a floor—say a wooden one, if handy—or in shallow boxes—in single depth with the crown ends up, and let them sprout an inch or so of strong shoots, and they will chiefly and most strongly sprout from the crown ends if placed as directed. It will be well to have them arranged before sprouting, farther than to show life; and when desirous to retard growth give light, and to increase and quicken, keep dark; and when the shoots are grown to the desired length, expose pretty fully to the light to allow the young shoots to strengthen before planting. To plant whole potatoes has been my almost invariable practice (unless when scarce of any sort and wishing to multiply), and I have no hesitation in saying that, as a rule, it is best, and especially with kidney sorts— which, if to be cut at all, should be done down the centre. By planting whole and well-shaped tubers of all varieties, I have found the crop, in nineteen cases out of twenty, to be decidedly the best for every purpose. A few hours at least before, or a day, or even two—but a few hours are sufficient to give time to stop bleeding and harden sufficiently before placing in the soil—cut off about a fourth part of the root end of each tuber to accelerate decay, for it is not good that the seed should remain fresh and sound too long in any case. Then with a pointed knife cut out to the roots and thoroughly, to prevent sprouting again, all the eyes, unless the strong shoots on the crown, of which leave one or two, or three according to sorts. . . . . I may remark that in these times of disease very late varieties are not to be commended, and scarcely to be risked at all.

"PLANTING.—For exhibition purposes I do not approve of, nor have I practised, early planting; and for any purpose, where there is the danger of spring frosts, if too soon above ground, great harm may result from being frosted down. Besides, I prefer rather not to plant till there is some natural heat in the soil and then the growth both below and above can proceed unchecked; and by speedy and unchecked growth, my impression is, that better and brighter samples for exhibition will be obtained. The greatest care (where there is such danger) should be taken to prevent frosting down in any case.

"Immediately before proceeding to plant, sow at the rate of say 4 cwt. of common or agricultural salt per acre, which is then worked through the soil in planting. I can recommend this as of great importance. Besides other beneficial results it tends to prevent to some extent the operations of worms, &c., and in dry weather conserves needed moisture, and in a wet season it does no harm.

"The next and most important matter is as to the manuring. If dung is to be used at all it will be best to have it put into the ground at the end of the year, and then it will be in good condition to be wrought through the soil when planting in spring, when artificial manure should only be used. If dung is to be used *when* planting, for prize growing, let it be pretty fresh, well-conditioned stable dung, comparatively free of litter, and used below, above, and around the sets, intermixed with the artificial manure and other materials that may be employed, taking care to have a little soil between the sets and the manures. My own practice, however, for years, from which I have obtained the best results, has been to grow without dung, and I shall simply and plainly describe my process of planting. . . . . I have used 27 in. between the drills in general, as the greatest distance, and about 12 in. between the sets, and these distances have given the most satisfactory results. There might be some variation made according to sorts, but I think it is little needed, for the varieties with small tops are in general most difficult to get to good size, and are therefore helped by plenty of space. . . . . It is good also, for fear of failure, in any way, not to plant all of one sort consecutively, or in one plot. . . . . Care must be taken that the small topped varieties shall not be so intermixed with the large as to get smothered, and it will be well if planting with the broad side of the drill to the mid-day sun (of which I most approve and have found best), to graduate the sorts according to size of haulms, beginning with the smallest at the south side of the plot.

"See to obtain a first-class artificial potato manure. . . . . That which I have found to answer better than any other I have tried for experiment alongside, is the Potato Manure, manufactured by Messrs. F. C. Hills & Co., Deptford and East Greenwich, and use at the rate of from 8 to 12 cwt. per acre, according to the nature of the soil and its previous manurial condition. Get to hand also a supply of pounded wood charcoal—that is, in a state of brokenness, in the particles ranging from the size of the grossest parts of crystallized sugar down to dust—and use at the rate of about 8 cwt. per acre. This is a most important factor in growing prize potatoes, and the bright and polished appearance of my exhibits has been the result in a great measure of the use of charcoal. Where the soil is not naturally sandy, it will be well to procure a quantity of sand—not too small-grained—to mix in the tuber-beds in planting. The use of sand will contribute not only to cleanness of growing, but to that attractive crackliness of skin especially peculiar to some sorts, and will also draw additional heat and keep an open tuber-bed.

"I shall now describe the process of planting, . . . I mean spade-planting proper; I disapprove wholly of dibbling. Beginning at the south side of the plot, dig over as much as gives sufficient breadth for one side of the drill, and a good portion to be taken down to the working side to have plenty of loose earth about the tubers, and to work up along with the manuring. Stretch a line and cut along with the spade, making a trench of about four inches deep (I prefer shallow planting). Throw in with the hand—spreading well and equally—a good application of the potato manure—a large handful to a yard, or more or less as required for the sort—and

with the spade strew over the manure as much soil
as lightly covers it. Then plant the sets, placing them
as far from the breast in front as allows the manuring,
&c., to be done as equally as possible all round, to
the extent required for a sufficient tuber-bed to each
set, and with the shoots lying or disposed towards
the sun. (This I generally have done, but it may
be a mere fancy.) Then with the hands cover over
the tubers and shoots carefully with loose, pure earth,
and strew around and over, a good handful of the
charcoal; then an application of sand—if the soil is
heavy or not particularly light—using a spadeful or
more to a yard of drill, or around and over three
sets. Then give a sprinkling of the manure, regulated in quantity according to sort. And if disposed
to be at the trouble, repeat the same process with
charcoal, sand, and manure, but first strewing some
friable mould over the manure before proceeding to
the second course. If to be done well or most perfectly, all the materials should be spread around
equally with the hand. . . . . A third similar
process even may be gone through, giving less of
manure and charcoal each time the oftener gone over,
and in all about the same quantity as in the first
application of each, and of sand *ad libitum* according
to soil. . . . . I prefer to plant without dung for
this reason, among others, that with manures only
there is less liability to disease, or if it attacks it will
be, as a rule, less virulent. Besides, dung tends
greatly to gather worms, and if it be correct (as
seems to me very probable) that scab is caused by

the common worm, then to use manure as I have described renders it almost impossible for worms to operate near the tubers, and thus scab, which mars so greatly for competition, may in great measure be prevented, as well as worm-holes, which destroy the potato to some extent for any purpose.

"When the haulms appear above ground, if there is any risk of frosting, it will be well to be very watchful, and if no other means of protection is handy, or if not inclined to be at the cost of other appliances, draw the earth over them when at night or early morning (before the sun appears) a dangerous freezing is observed.

"EARTHING-UP may be done at once or twice. If twice, the first earthing should be when the haulms are about 4 in. above the level surface, and the second when 3 to 4 in. farther advanced. Before the second earthing up, if the ground is not in very fine working order, dig between the drills with a four-tined steel fork. By this process the ground is better pulverized, and the drills more easily and perfectly formed. If the complete earthing-up is to be done at once, let it be before the haulms exceed 6 to 8 in. high, taking care not to cover the leaves, and to a whole depth of about 9 in. counting from where the earth is drawn, and leaving the top of ridge at least 5 in. broad. . . . . The crop may sometimes appear much in need of watering; but I have rarely had recourse to it, except at times to assist the swelling of samples for early exhibitions."

EXHIBITING.—The department of exhibiting consists mainly of selection, dress, and show, into which Mr. Porter goes minutely. He says: "Want of skill or carelessness in selecting, may render the very best productions unsuccessful. Uniformity in the size and type of the tubers of each dish, is of the utmost moment, combined with the greatest perfection in form, beauty, and freedom from defect. There must be at least two selectings. First, roughly in digging and before washing, and then more carefully after, as the washing often reveals faults unobserved before. If a great deal of work has to be gone through, occupying days or, perhaps, a week or more, great care should be taken to preserve the tubers fresh, and to secure this, the digging, selecting, washing, and re-selecting, and laying away from the light, or covering closely and thoroughly, should be done with the utmost despatch as well as efficiency. . . . . It may be expected that I should say something under this head as to sizes of tubers. No rule can well be laid down on this point. Common sense, observation, and practice, must in a great measure be the teachers here; and sizes may be accounted large or small, or medium relatively, and according to sorts. . . . . One dish may pretty safely be trusted, however, if the samples are large, or above what might be called medium size, and surpassingly beautiful, and absolutely perfect. Notwithstanding the cry by some for the exhibition of sizes suitable for a gentleman's table, it may be given as a general hint that tubers if really models as to shape, combined with fineness—that is, with shallow eyes and general beauty, and altogether approaching as near as possible to perfection, can scarcely be too large —if not absolute monsters, to find favour with judges as a rule.

"Dress.—Under the head 'dress' in my vocabulary, it should refer only to washing thoroughly, and removing any remaining part of string at root end of tuber, or anything else that may properly be tidied without coming under the appellation of artificial work—such as scraping off scab, plugging up worm-holes, or other defects, or greasing, so as to improve and conserve colour, which thus becomes unnatural, or polishing; all these are to be denounced, and should be disallowed; and it is well that judges are beginning to look with disfavour upon such artificial work. . . . . Some use as a finish soapy water, and it certainly will more fully cleanse than the pure cold water, and has a most pleasing effect on white potatoes in particular, by producing or increasing a charming delicacy of whiteness, and by the use of the soapy water there is no unpleasant effect either as to smell or the preservation of the tubers for any length of time for exhibition, even although they are not wiped, but left to dry of themselves. Using soapy water can scarcely be termed an artificial dressing, as it really is only a more perfect cleansing.

"I have seen various methods suggested of preserving the tubers fresh and fair after washing, but I know of no better plan than to lay them aside and keep them thoroughly in the dark; and when ready to pack to carry to the place of exhibition roll each separate tuber in a paper, and add a second one if thought necessary to prevent chafing, and arrange so as to prevent mixing of sorts. . . . Another thing to bear in mind is that while potatoes are so liable to disease it is necessary to have more than the required number of tubers of each sort packed, and in numbers varying according to the liability of the various sorts to go wrong after digging, and without any spot appearing even when washed. This is one very grievous effect of the scourge to the exhibitor, in creating additional work and added loads to carry. According to the greater or less virulence of the disease the extra tubers must be more or fewer. For some sorts, even in the worst seasons, one or two, or three extra at most, may be sufficient, while with others, such as 'Red Emperor,' there can be no assurance with even double the number required. I have instead of 9 laid by 15 of Emperor, all seeming quite sound when washed, and in a day or two found 10 of the 15 showing more or less unmistakable marks of disease, and unfit for exhibition.

"Snow.—As to this I have to remark that it is highly important to show well, that is to stage well, to arrange with taste, and with the best effect, so as to give a pleasing impression, and attract the eyes of the judges at first sight, and thus secure a more ready and narrow inspection." As we gave at the commencement of this volume a list of many varieties that the author considers well suited for exhibition, we will not refer further to the subject here, but conclude with a few observations that appeared in the *Gardeners' Magazine* of October, 1876, upon the Potato Show held that year, as follows:—" The beauty of Mr. Porter's winning lots was marvellous, and the question was asked by not a few, 'How could such growth and colour be obtained?' When assured that a kindly soil and a skilful cultivator were needed to ensure such results, 'they didn't seem to see it;' and that is the way of the world, to think that the results of years of work and thought can be conveyed to the utterly ignorant by some Abracadabra. Finer samples than Mr. Porter's have never been seen; at all events, no one living who has made systematic observation, say for a quarter of a century or so, has seen their equal, and we cannot expect in the future that they will be surpassed. There was never more satisfactory judging than in this case."

INDEX.

A

AUTUMN manuring, 17
    planting inadvisable, 39
    planting experiments by James Howard, M.P., 40

B

BLIGHT, how spread, 34
Blooming and fruiting, 96

C

CELLARS good for storing, 84
Chats, 80
Clamping, 81
    in Kent, 83
Clamps, lime in, 84
Cultivation, &c., in Scotland, 139
Culture, earlies, in Lancashire, 149
    earlies, in Scotland, 131
    for exhibition, 162
    increase of, in Jersey, 162
    in fields, 48
    in Jersey, 158
    in London market gardens, 127

Culture, main crops in Scotland, 137

D

DEPTH to plant, 37
Dibbling, 14
Digging, best time for, 75
    weather for, 82
Disease, cause of, 55
    different opinions respecting, 61
    Dr. Lang on, 71
    first appearance, 52
    first indications, 50
    high earthing preventive of, 66
    how promoted, 51
    Mr. Jensen's experiments, 67
    Mr. Jensen's remedies, 69
    Mr. Jensen's theory, 65
    Mr. John Friar on, 73
    Mr. Smith's evidence, 52
    prevention and palliation, 58
    remedies suggested, 63
    superphosphate as a preventive, 63
    to grapple with, 61
    ubiquity of spores, 60
Distance between rows, 35

E

EARLY sorts, 2
Earthing, 46
Exhibiting, 171
Expenses and returns, 129
Experiments, 112
    advantages of changing seed, 124
    conditions to be observed, 119
    influence of manures, 125
    on disease-resisting powers, 117
    on productive powers, 117
    summary of results, 126
    uses of, 113
    value of sundry manures, 120

F

FLUCTUATIONS, of trade, 160
Forcing, 105

G

GARDEN culture, 48

H

HANDLING unripe potatoes, 80
Harvesting in Scotland, 135
    late sorts in Scotland, 143
Horse hoeing, 44
How to "show" well, 173

I

INTER-CROPPING, 128

K

KIDNEYS for frame culture, 109

L

LATE sorts, 4
Laying down the haulm, 74
Lifting crops, 76
    machine for, 77

M

MANURE indispensable, 12
    where to place, 18
Manures, 15
    kainit, 120
    mineral superphosphate, 120
    nitrate of sodium, 120
    sulphate of ammonia, 120
Marketing, 78
    considerations respecting, 79
Mealiness and manures, 104
Modes of growing, 13
Mould-board plough, 134
Mr. Porter's prize exhibits, 174

N

NEW varieties, Scotch propagation of, 91

O

ORIGIN, 1

P

Packing up, 80
Planting and earthing up, 37
    best time for, 38
    in drills, 15
    in frames, 107
    Scotch preparation of land, 133
Ploughing in sets, 15
Potato selection, 102
Potatoes, a clergyman on, 8
    after ley, 141
    as a cleaning crop, 13
    as a paying crop, 131
    conveyance to St. Helier's, 161
    deteriorating, 103
    digging in Jersey, 161
    important crop in Jersey, 159
    important crop in Scotland, 148
Preparing ground, 11
Prices in Scotland, 136, 146
Productive powers, 2

R

Root-houses and cellars, 83
Root-warmth and top heat, 108

S

Sale of earlies in Lancashire, 157
Saving valuable time, 142
Screens, 149
Second earlies, 4
Seed-balls, 95
Seed changing, 141
    choice of, 23
    Director Sturtevant on cutting, 114
    disposal of surplus, 111
    potatoes, 20
    storing on shelves, 89
    to obtain, 21
    weight per acre, 42
Seedlings, American treatment of, 94
    Messrs Bliss on raising, 100
    raising, 90
Seeds sowing, 92
    to select, 97
Sets, 22
    cutting, 25
    cutting, in Scotland, 140
    cutting kidney, 26
    distance between, 35
    experiments in cutting, 28
    knife for cutting, 83
    lying thinly, 11
    whole or cut, 27
"Show" potatoes, dressing, 172
    earthing, 170
    manure for, 167
    planting, 166
    preserving, 172
    salt for, 166
    seed, 164
    soil for, 163
Site for frames, 106
    for potatoes, 44
Soil, Middlesex, and flavour, 104

Soils, 6
  change of, 19
  in Scotland, 138
  Shirley Hibberd on, 9
Sorts for main Scotch crop, 144
  some good, 105
Spade-planting, for "Show" potatoes, 168
Spring frosts, 43
Storing, 56
  American system, 85
  determined by the quantity, 88

T

TEMPORARY frame, 109
Thinning the haulm, 45
Trestles for frames, 151
Turf pits, 153
Twenty-four varieties, 6

W

WIDE planting and intercropping, 36
Wintering potatoes, 87
Wire-worms, 7
  protection against, 38
World-wide cultivation, 11

THE END.

www.ingramcontent.com/pod-product-compliance
Lightning Source LLC
Chambersburg PA
CBHW020249170426
43202CB00008B/290